REBIRTH & REVIVAL

OF A REBEL

Inspirational – Transformational - Motivational

The True Story Of A Former Criminal Who
Has Discovered The Path To His Positive
Influential Identity While In Prison

JEAN BELIZAIRE
Author & Pastor

FORWARD

There is no greater witness to truth of the gospel than the evidence of a life that has been and is being transformed by its unique message. Within these pages you will read of one such person whose life has been dramatically changed through the message of the gospel of the Lord Jesus Christ. It has been and continues to be my privilege to witness this transformation first hand!

I first met Jean as a young man committed to the (DCJDC) Department of Corrections Juvenile Detention Center in Dorchester Massachusetts. Although I have personally witnessed to hundreds of young men in this situation, I have rarely had the opportunity to maintain contact with these individuals long after their incarceration.

I truly count it a privilege to have shared the gospel with Jean and to watch him grow and develop into a mighty man of God anointed to preach, teach and proclaim the message of the Lord Jesus Christ to his community and around the world.

As you read this riveting story of his journey, I pray that you will substantially be inspired and motivated to know the ONE who he has met and invite HIM to lead you on your own personal journey!

His Servant,
Richard Williamson

Chapter One
Where it all begins

I was born to two Haitian immigrants who voyaged from Petite Goave, Haiti to the city of Brockton, Massachusetts. The way my parents met was a bit on the unusual side. My mother first came to the U.S to live with an aunt that lived in Brockton. My mother was initially introduced to my father through a photograph. She found him attractive, so an arrangement was made for them to communicate and meet. Even though we know that it is ideal to get to know a person before we embark on a journey in a relationship, most of the time we bypass protocol, and when we bypass protocol, we always end up in deep waters, waters that we fight for a lifetime to get out of, just as in the case with my mother's marriage to my father.

Father Ke'bo was the Catholic Priest who married my parents. He was known to be a stern man, a no-nonsense type of fellow who expected order and organization in everything he did.

Many people felt that this marriage would not last. They just did not see longevity in the cards for my folks. The priest even had his reservations, but he united them in holy matrimony anyway. My father already had three children, but my mother was only told about two when they initially met.

My mother was a virgin when they married and had grown up in a strict religious home raised by devout Catholic family members. My mother never really knew her father and her mother died shortly after I was born. My father never knew his dad either, because he died when my father was 3.

Back in Haiti, my father played soccer, was in a jazz band, and worked with his hands doing various things. He voyaged to the United States in 1975 to reside with my mother. In May of 1978, I was born and, in the following year, my brother was born.

So the genesis of me began with me being born to two Haitian immigrants in search of a better life, missing their homeland at times, but seeking to adjust and pursue a better way for themselves.

As I was growing up, my mother would often tell me how happy my father was that I had come into this world. I carried his first name, but not with Jr added. He named my brother and I after Catholic saints. My middle name, Patrick, was named after St. Patrick and my brother was named Jude after St. Jude. My father was brought up Catholic, but his religion was more occultist, if anything. As I began to discover more and more, my senses grew and my curiosity caused me to inquire about certain things.

My father was always a stern and stubborn man, hardworking and didn't seem to have too many friends. The older he got, the smaller his circle became. I attributed that to his temper and reckless speech, but from what my mom said, he had high expectations for me. It was never really clear what they were, but my arrival into this world made him feel good. I was considered his firstborn.

I think any man in this world would be happy to have a son because there is so much a man can do, in terms of pouring into his sonand leaving an imprint on his life. I think that's why I shared his name.

Later in life, I would wonder if there was any special reason as to why I was named after a Catholic saint since I believe that names have prophetic meaning. My father engaged in occultist practices, so I naturally wondered if I was named after the Voudu Loa Damballa, who in Vodouisant syncretism, is represented by SaintPatrick.

Growing up, I was always an ambitious kid taking books from the library to read about athletes that achieved their fame due to their various achievements. I think I read up on every sport there was because I bounced from one idea to another in terms of what I wanted to be when I grew up. I think most kids do that anyhow. Even though I researched various sports, basketball seemed to be my niche. I played church league basketball, attempted junior high and, eventually, high school teams, but always quit.

As I grew up, reading became one of my strengths, and, as a result, it affected my cognition and made me a better thinker.

Since I had a great memory, which can be a gift and a curse, I could read a book and remember most of its information. It would later make me a very versatile person in terms of relating to others. I could have conversations with different people on different subjects, never felt boxed in and it gave me great vocabulary skills that I use today.

I excelled in school when I wanted to and applied myself, but I was told early on by teachers, coaches, authorities and the like that I had one of the worst attitudes they had ever seen. I really don't know what contributed to my attitude problem. I grew up with both parents in the home, unlike most black men. My parents tried to instill some morals in my siblings and I. For the most part, I had a happy childhood, but there were still downsides, especially regarding my parents. My dad was a compulsive gambler. My mom was too passive, tolerated his poor financial decisions and never liked it when we brought up his gambling because she didn't want to admit that he had a problem. He was also a flagrant womanizer and it hurt me to know my mother was constantly getting hurt by his lack of faithfulness, but she was still passive and silent. Nevertheless, they stayed together. I guess that stands for something, at least I hoped.

I think it's good to be passive and hold one's peace in certain regards, but in the case of my mother, she held her peace so much, that she had no voice when it came to dealing with my father. I think that is the danger of being too tolerant and passive because, as a result, one loses his or her voice.

I mentioned earlier that my father had three kids prior to marrying my mom. My brother and I were born before all my sisters came from Haiti. Life at home was ok with just my brother and I. We were close and I picked on him a lot just as big brothers do. As we got older, we drifted apart. I attributed that to being out of his life for nearly 6 years because I did time in a penal institution.

My parents were steadfast in their love for us, trying not to show partiality even though that's not humanly possible, made sure our needs were met and that they were proactive in our lives. My sisters were back in Haiti. I can recall my parents recording messages on cassette tapes to send to them and vice versa. Looking back, it's strange to even mention cassette tapes since they don't exist anymore!

I can recall looking forward to the day they would come to the U.S and we would meet them in person, but of course, as sibling rivalry would be sure to ensue, my brother and I would later be jealous of them coming because they received preferential treatment from my dad.

I didn't have a lot of friends at a very young age. I was the type of kid that was picked on in school because of what I wore, so I never really fit in with the crowd. My parents were hard working people that did not believe in spoiling us with expensive tennis shoes and clothing. When the school year began, we could only pick out a few things, but the budget was slim, so we fussed and complained over stuff we wanted, but couldn't get.

As I got older, I realized my parents were both good providers but, at a young age, I always felt and wanted them to do more. I had a total lack of understanding on my part and I was operating with limited view.

I can remember being bullied in school, kids always wanting to fight and me running home from school so that I wouldn't be ganged up on. Later in life, because I would do time in prison and adjust to the atmosphere of prison, I would quickly develop a no-nonsense, I fear no man, I fear nothing, only the power of God, mentality.

I understood that different environments breed certain mindsets and behaviors. Prison cultivates a specific type of mindset, especially if you have to be there for a long time. You don't have the mindset of a citizen because you are not in the free world. You are in the world with the worst of the worst and if you are among lions, then you must be a lion to survive. If you are a sheep, then you will be devoured. I learned that pretty quickly.

I did have one close friend as a kid, whose name I won't mention for confidentiality purposes. We played basketball together all the time and I became his friend, oddly enough, after we got into a fight at school. We became great friends after that, hanging out after school, talking frequently about girls in school we liked, etc.

It's funny how life accelerated for us, how we went from doing innocent things to things that were criminal in nature. It makes one wonder what went wrong and propelled us to make the choices we made and take the paths we took. I guess we can never predict what life will bring. Both our lives did not change for the better. I introduced him to weed and we started to smoke it together.

When I would go to prison, he was the only one from my small group of teenage friends that would keep it solid with me. He accepted my calls from jail and would pay out of pocket for the costs. However, when I came home from my sentence, he was heavily involved with the drug life, hustling cocaine, weed and the like. I, on the other hand, had different goals that were more spiritual in nature and the goal was to never go back to prison again.

After a while, I gained acceptance from kids in school. I started hanging with a group of guys after school. We would meet up and all chip in for weed. I was a positive kid overall with a high intellect so this created a big crisis.

Chapter Two
Man in crisis

Like most teenage kids, I was looking for my niche, my niche in terms of friends, dreams, girls etc. I can remember getting rides from my dad to church league basketball games. I've always known my parents to be supportive, but couldn't understand why he or my mother never came to my games. It was hard to explain to my teammates and coach why my parents weren't there. I've concluded that it was more of a cultural thing rather than them being unsupportive, but it did hurt, especially if I did well in a game and they were not there to celebrate with me.

But I mentioned the rides to the games and, on my way to the games, I saw kids I knew from school. They were the popular kids, who were known for being tough, fighting, and getting into trouble. I knew their names and who they were. They would be standing on street corners selling drugs or "pumping" as they called it back then, for known dealers. I remember being fascinated as my dad's car drove into these areas and I noticed these kids. They seemed cool. They had the expensive sneakers, jewelry and hip-hop culture clothing.

I wanted to be like them, dress like them, have money like them, even be the center of attention like them. Even though I heard stories of them getting robbed, losing the people that they were selling formoney, getting locked up and sometimes having the people they were "pumping" for turn on them in the blink of an eye, I still wanted to be like them.

Deep inside, I wasn't happy with who I was. I had a warm home to go to, some friends, etc, but I was still looking for some sort of purpose. The things I was trying, like basketball, wasn't working out because I didn't follow through and, grade wise, I wasn't up to par.

I remember meeting one kid who was hustling for a guy. He told me he was about to go out on his own and he would need someone to "pump" for him. He said he liked me and thought I'd be good. It never worked out between me and him. Later on in life, he would be successful at the drug trade.

Soon after I met this boy, I met a kid who came to my school. Immediately, he was the talk of school because he had custom made outfits and jewelry. He brought guns to school and had the prettiest girl in the school in no time.

He asked some of my friends about me and they vouched for me. We would say what's up to each other in school and he thought I was cool. I would later find out from them that he wanted me to "pump" for him, but wanted to make sure I was solid before approaching me.

He had quite the reputation. He was known to police, had beef with kids that had street cred, had been shot at a young age and had been selling drugs since he was twelve.

So I started out with him. One day after school, another kid he recruited and I stopped by his home to pick up crack to sell. In those days, you could have 20 people on the street corners of Brockton flagrantly standing out there selling drugs. The crack epidemic was huge. It was known to everyone and everyone would get their money.

I remember the first time I went out to sell. I was psyching myself up to go out on the corner. We stopped by the kid's aunt's house who I was selling for and we waited there for a while. I wanted so bad to hustle, not so much for the money, but more for the reputation. I remember his brother showing off a TEC (semi-automatic) to us that he had under a mattress.

We went out to the corner and the first car that pulled up was my elementary school teacher. It was her and a man she was with asking for crack. It was dark out so I recognized her, but she did not recognize me. I'll never forget the feeling that came over me as I realized the reality that crack cocaine really ravages lives. Even my elementary substitute teacher was hooked. It was then that I realized the power drugs can have over one's life.

The kid who recruited me liked me a lot over the other kid he had recruited because I was more committed than him. He had plans for me to be a fellow partner. One of the other partners took me on the handle of a bike while being "out on the block ", as they called it. He told me to keep the money and come so we could get jewels, gear, honeys, money, straps and all that.

I can remember feeling, as I was on the handle of that bike like, I was making it. I was a "shorty on the block", as they called me. I was catching the attention of certain peers and felt like I was accomplishing some goals. I really didn't know what I was doing on the block at first, but who does when they first step out? I just knew that I was in a serious atmosphere so I had to be serious because the environment dictated it.

My parents had no clue that I was sneaking drugs into their home and didn't know what I was doing when I stepped out of the house. They weren't neglectful parents and they did the very best they could. I just think they were too busy working and did not see that I was getting in deeper and deeper, deeper than not excelling in school, deeper than just arguing back with them over things and being disrespectful to them.

I will never forget this particular day when I was out there on the block I had sold all the "work" (product) I was sent out there with. I was socializing a little and decided I was going to leave. There was something about that night that me feel like it was going to be different, almost like something was about to go down, as Spider-Man would say "My spidey senses" were kicking in.

I left and, ten minutes after, the block was raided. There was a lot of cocaine and weed being pushed off of this particular street. Everyone that was trying to get a piece of the pie was out there, at least those that were accepted to come out there. I had got word about it shortly after. It made me a little nervous about going out.

I remember going to my room placing a call to a close friend and telling him how the block got raided, how this dealer loved me, and saw a future with me in it as an associate. However, I still wanted to play basketball and I was a little worried about getting caught up seeing that I was getting in deep real fast. He told me, "If I were you, I would tell him you are not interested anymore." I then made the call to the person I was running for (selling).

I told him I wasn't interested anymore. He told me it was cool, but I found out from his girl that it wasn't cool, especially when I noticed his demeanor became different towards me. She let me know that he was always praising me up and telling people I was his right-hand man. Then I told him I didn't want to go out anymore, and he was taken aback by that.

I guess it was because I came across so committed. He didn't perceive that I was having second thoughts, especially after that big raid where just about everyone got picked up. Looking back, I don't regret backing out because this same person, years later, would create a lot of enemies, and be killed in a club out of state.

Some people said it was the result of bad karma, that he and others showed off too much and that he had beef with too many people. I could see it coming too. He walked around sometimes with a bulletproof vest and that showed how endangered his life had become.

Chapter Three
Thirsting for a Reputation

Even though I was looking to escape the lure of the street, I was still being pulled back. I was still smoking weed and affiliating with those that dabbled in drug dealing, but I hadn't been dealing for a little while. At that time, there was news spreading all around town about these kids that became "stick up kids" and were robbing everyone and everything in sight. I first heard a rumor about a sneaker truck that was robbed at gunpoint, then at a gun store and then a bank.

One of the kids I went to school with was a year older than me. I would see him in school, but it was mainly in the hallways or in detention hall. He dropped out of school, and the word around the school was that he was running with this notorious group of kids who everyone feared and they were talking about them and the latest news.

I began to have an obsession with this group and I wanted to be like these guys. For me, it wasn't so much about the money as much it was about a reputation. So, I was up on the latest news with them and, even though I had left drug dealing, I acquired new goals in the life of crime. I wanted a reputation as a "stick up kid". The problem was that I lost access to guns when I left the kid I used to deal for and I didn't have one of my own at the time. I tried hard to find one at that time, but everyone who said they were going to sell one to me backed out of it even though I knew they could legitimately sell me one. Also, the people I contacted had guns. They just didn't sell me one.

Looking back, it was an act of God because a gun in the hand of a person seeking a reputation is a very dangerous thing.

I repeat, a very dangerous thing. I remember one day getting hold of a Slick Rick tape and hearing the song "Children's Story". I played it over and over again. I did not necessarily blame my actions on the music, but something about the character in the song robbing people, like he had a disease, appealed to me and reassured me even more that I wanted to be a "stick up kid".

I remember in 1993 when Snoop Doggy Dogg was a big hit. His album, "Doggystyle", was being played and talked about everywhere. I was a fan and there was something eerie about the album, especially the song "Murder was the Case" that even to this day brings me back to scary visions of how I used to be at the time the album dropped.

I guess when I hear it today, I can recall being in a bad place mentally, a very dangerous place to be exact. I was a danger to myself and especially others. I desired a rep and started to make moves in that regard. The guys I hung with started to call me "sticky short" for sticky fingers. I liked the name and loved when people greeted me by that name. When others found out about it, other people started calling me that.

I started to meet different people. One of the kids I started hanging with was a cousin to one of the "stick up kids" I mentioned earlier that was terrorizing the city. He was not a significant part of my life. Our friendship was mainly smoking weed every day. Because of my strange way of thinking, I hung out with him anyway because he was first cousin to one of the kids I was idolizing. I felt by hanging with him, I was getting closer to his cousins, but his cousin got killed over a jacket he had robbed someone for. Apparently, he wanted the jacket from a friend and threatened his friend, and that same friend came back with the jacket, but under was a gun and he shot three pe that were in the house, killing two and wo ling one. I continued to idolize him even after his death.

I craved a rep and would do anything to get it. I can remember telling a guy about my mission one time. He brought up this kid, and he was trying to talk some sense into me pointing out how he died. He was speaking from an older person point of view. I was 15 at the time and was hardened very quickly, seeing only my street fantasies.

I laughed as he spoke to me while I was in a friend's room smoking a blunt, the kind of laugh that was sinister, the kind that had nothing to lose. The reality was that I had a lot to lose, but was getting deep so fast, that I was reckless. I saw death in the line of my mission as glory and a badge of honor.

Chapter Four
Havoc

It is a very scary thing when one is no longer sensitive to right and wrong. It is a bad place to be when your mind is warped and you begin to see wrong as right and right as wrong. It is a cold state of mind that one has when you play Russian roulette with your life, and the lives of others become a sport to you. You are in the devil's world practicing his work and are a conduit for havoc.

By the time I was a freshman in high school, I was in a place in my mind where I fantasized about creating havoc and, 9 times out of 10, when you think about something so much and for too long, you eventually act on it. Freshman year, I was arrested on Veterans Day for 5 counts of assault and battery. A melee, or a confused fight, had occurred on a bridge where myself and three codefendants, all close friends, got into a fight with some kids that were staring at us too long and hard. We had weapons, and before you know it, there was a brawl in the middle of the street. My friend was accused of stabbing a guy, an older guy nearly twice his age. We were all 15 at the time and, my friend accused of the stabbing, would later in life be deported from the U.S to Cape Verde along with my other two codefendants. He would be charged later in life with murder out there. He did about 14 years and got killed there.

Rumors going around said it was because he was good with his hands. He was a fighter and people were jealous that he was scrapping it out with people and coming out on top, so they killed him.

After I went to prison, one of them would get shot in the face by an enemy and the other deported for being a part of crime wave.

Looking back, there was the spirit of death on the lifestyle my associations and I lived. When you are walking in a life a crime, things don't end well. There are only a few that change their lives or turn to religion for saving grace.

I was bailed out the night I caught my first case. My parents believed the lies I told them about what happened that night. I made it seem like we were victims when we were actually instigators of the whole thing. I went back to school and didn't skip a beat, but I cared less for school at this point. I was coming to class high, selling weed in school, and chasing every girl that moved.

My priorities became much more different. Meanwhile, my mind was continuing to grow darker and darker. I became very violent because I wanted to prove the notion that I was "ill", as they called it on the streets, that

I was crazy, and that there was nobody more "iller" than me.

Then, in May of 1994, I was with a friend. We made a habit of meeting up after school to smoke weed. He had dropped out of school and his mother knew we smoked weed. In fact, she actually smoked with us at times. She was cool with us smoking at her house and sometimes she would tell us that she'd rather see us smoke weed than that "white stuff ", meaning crack cocaine.

I always found that out of place because of how my parents raised me. I smoked weed with a couple of my friend's mothers who didn't care, but I noticed that this was something I couldn't do with my parents. Later on in life, I would see that I was blessed to have good parents, not perfect, but good.

The kid and I wanted to smoke weed, but we had no money. I got a hold of three dollars and we went to the another side of town to see if some people we used to" catch sessions" with (smoke weed) had weed. When we got there, as soon as we walked through the door, they asked if we had weed.

We replied that we came there thinking they might have some and I let them know I had three dollars and asked if someone could go to the liquor store and get a 64 ounce of private stock for three dollars. A girl in the house was willing to go. She was 21 and I was kind of feeling her and wanted to sleep with her, but the time and place were never right.

She said she'd go to the store with some form of ID. So the girl drove the kid and I to the liquor store. On our way, a conversation struck up about robbing someone one, not sure who started it, but I was definitely down for it, after all, that was my expertise.

We talked about having her go into a bar and lure a person out to rob them. We made an attempt to implement this plan, but it fell through because she got nervous. There was also talk about someone in the neighborhood that was selling us a gun. I got excited about that. After I fell out of contact with the kid that I sold drugs for, I lost access to guns, and no one would sell me one, which like I said, was a blessing I would discover later in life .

I always wanted a strap, which was a holster. I felt it would help me be more successful in my robbing sprees. I wanted to rob a gun store like the kids I idolized. I felt that I was a worthy "stick up kid". The girl and I went to the liquor store and the conversation continued. There was also a bet that I wouldn't have the heart to stab someone, and I was itching to prove that I would.

There was something about when I was in crowds that made me amped up to show that I was that crazy dude I thirsted to be known as.

It's a danger to try to prove yourself because when you try to prove yourself, you lose yourself and I was getting ready to lose big time. I was getting ready to lose a significant part of my life by serving an 8-10 year prison sentence in the Massachusetts Department of Corrections. I remember we went to the liquor store, but the girl we were with was denied because something was wrong with her I.D.

I was outside smoking a cigarette and I noticed this girl in a BMW staring in my direction. Later, this same woman would testify that she saw me in the area the night when the robbery and stabbing occurred. We walked past another store and there was a key in the ignition of a car and the car was running with the doors unlocked. We thought of stealing it. Something about that night made us all itching to do something wrong. We were up to no good, and when you are looking for trouble, it's not hard to find. Sometimes, trouble approaches you, but when you are geared towards mischief, it will be happy to introduce himself to you.

I remember this older guy being with us that night. I didn't know him too well and this was only my second time with him. I had smoked a couple blunts with him once before. The apartment we were at was his, and we were welcomed in again that night because the mutual connection was the girl who we went to the liquor store with.

Everything happened so fast that night but, when you are young and living fast, you learn to keep up with the pace. You also learn pretty quickly that you will eventually self-destruct, and you will crash and burn hard. All I remember is that I saw a woman approaching her car.

I ran up to her and started to stab her from behind. I thought it was only two times but, later on, police reports would say that she suffered three stab wounds and her lungs collapsed in the process. I recall being in court one time and seeing the pictures of blood all over and inside her car. It was havoc, signs of the havoc my mind had fantasized about. I pulled the strap from her purse and it broke. The purse fell to the ground, I picked it up and started to run through this grocery store parking lot in broad daylight.

I remember there was a little boy. The police reports described him as her great-grandson. I ran towards a wooded area, ducking people that tried to stop me. I have never had I run so hard in my life before. I opened up the purse and there was $83.00 in there with some credit cards. I ditched the knife, purse and cards and ran through a little league baseball field where a baseball game was happening.

I remember some guy helping me to find my way back to the apartment. He was a Spanish guy that said, "Aqui" to me on Spanish, meaning "here". When I got into the house, the others I was with had found their way back there. I remember threatening to commit suicide if the police came to get me. There was the sound of sirens everywhere.

I was asking them to contact the guy who supposedly had 40 calibers for sale. I was asked how much money I had. I told everyone. They knew someone who sold weed. They came over and served us an ounce of weed with the money. I was told if I smoked a joint, I would feel better.

The guy that was supposed to sell me the gun came in and said somebody just stabbed an old lady and the cops are everywhere. Someone in the house pointed to me and said I was the one who did it.

He said that he would not come over with any guns because the block was too was hot, which made sense. I remember being at the point where murder became my initial instinct. I was hoping that he would come with the gun and do something foolish like hand it to me loaded.

To this day, I believe I would've shot him in the head, but he didn't bring the gun. I changed my clothes while I was there, left my jacket at the house, broke off some bud (weed) to the dude that owned the apartment and took a Brockton yellow cab home.

After I bought an ounce of weed, I had little money for the cab. One thing I remember about the cab ride was the taxi cab driver was talking about the stabbing and robbery and didn't realize that he was driving the one who just did it.

There was a guy who came over to the house that knew about it as well. I got home and asked my mother for the remainder of the money for the cab because the driver was waiting outside for me. I paid him and I remember my mother asking me where the new jacket she had bought me was. I lied to her and told her I was at the YMCA playing basketball and left it there. She chastised me about the jacket. It was a pinstripe throwback Chicago White Sox jacket. It was nice and quite noticeable to anyone who would wear it. I told her I'd go to the YMCA the next day to get it. It was actually at the apartment I was at not too long ago.

I remember going to my room where I shared a bed with my younger brother. I remember looking at the ounce of weed I bought, smelling it and saying to myself that I had the connection on some good weed. This sparked an idea that I could start hustling weed. I thought about my peers in school that I could serve (sell to). Surprisingly, after all that had just recently occurred, I still fell asleep that night.

Thinking back, I thought it was crazy how I could nearly take someone's life and go to sleep like nothing happened, but when you create havoc, you have no problem with it. It becomes a part of you, just a normal part of life. Havoc is a familiar face and friend on the streets, only havoc is not a friend because, in the end, those who practice havoc are succumbed to the dangerous consequences of this "religion".

I say religion because, religiously, I practiced havoc. It was a very cold truth, but true, nonetheless the very next day, I went through town letting some friends know that I had a good weed connection. I came home and two friends greeted me outside of my house. One of them had a 40 ounce for me and one for him. We went to his house and began to break up and bag the weed. We rolled two blunts and started to smoke and it hit me pretty hard. I think it was Thai Stick chocolate, which is very strong.

A newspaper delivery boy came to deliver the paper to my friend's house .The headline in the paper said that a 73-year-old great grandmother was stabbed in the grocery store parking lot. I remembered laughing to myself and saying to the others in the house with me "I'm a celebrity now ".

In my warped way of thinking, I believed that I was earning a reputation, but what I really hungered for a purpose, but I was finding my purpose in a criminal lifestyle.

That day, I was higher than I have ever been before. I remember twisting the cap of the 40 ounce of Olde English Ale, but never taking a sip. The weed put me into a comatose state. It was like I heard the voice of God in the middle of my high saying to me, "You are going to get locked up today."

I made it home and tried to sleep my high off. When I walked home, my parents had a copy of the newspaper on the dining room table. I vaguely remember them talking about the headlines. Little did they know, the culprit of the crime was their son, a son they had raised right, but had deviated from their principles, not because they did not do their best, but because their son was enamored with a life that really was no life at all and would soon find that out behind concrete walls and razor wire.

That night, I slept off my high in the same bed I shared with my brother and, in the middle of the night, my house was surrounded by police cruisers and K9's. The police read me my Miranda rights. I remember being taken away while neighbors looked to see what was going on with all the flashing lights and police cars, and as the cop car drove off with me in cuffs, I knew, in a very real way, that it would be a very long time before I saw my neighborhood again, my stomping ground and the free world.

Chapter Five
Rain Drops

The police brought me to the station for booking. I was handcuffed to a railing at the city station. I remember an officer talking to me, and saying how I should know that lady could very likely die. I replied, "I'm sorry to hear that, but I didn't do it." My heart was calloused and cold from the odyssey, which was the criminal underworld took me on and the change happened in me when I became fascinated with its deviance and magnetism.

There were a lot of officers dying to get a look at me while I was being booked and held in a holding cell. My original bail was $100,000. Even with the bail set that high and the fact that I was brought in by the cops, somewhere in my young mind, it still did not yet register that I was in deep trouble.

After the arraignment, the court officers were getting me ready to leave the court. I was last to go on the paddy wagon. When I stepped out the courthouse, there were news cameras all over, and this kid I knew who was on trial for murder, and was already in the wagon yelled, "Flip em the bird." I just shuffled out to the wagon. It was a long ride that night, the longest I ever had going back and forth to court.

I can remember people on the wagon saying that the lady had died. In my mind, I said that I'm officially a murderer now. I was relieved, however, to find out it wasn't true. Looking back, I'm happy that I didn't take that woman's life. We both were spared by that, but more her than me.

When I went into the Department of Youth center in Roslindale, I can recall the staff strip searching me saying, "The guys in here heard about what you did. Most of them didn't see you on TV, so I want you to say that you are in here for gun possession, that you got caught with a 38 caliber handgun."

I went along with that for a few days because that's what I was told and I had never been incarcerated for anything before. However, I couldn't keep up the front at first. I was scared because I had never been locked before.

Here I was at 15 years of age, just 7 days before my 16th birthday. I soon realized I had to stand up for myself and not let anyone run all over me because I had enough sense by this time to realize that I'd be there for a little while.

So, I got into fights and soon challenged those who challenged me and, eventually, I was seen as a cool dude, but what I did was a heinous crime and there seemed to be, amongst my peers, a separation and distinction between the two.

I got depressed and contemplated suicide. The stress became unmanageable. The realization of how deep this situation became happened when I heard my dad crying on the phone after finding out where they had sent me from the courthouse.

I had never really heard him cry before, except when my grandmother died. I cried some nights in my cell. Not certain of my future, my attorney told me the prosecutor was looking to try me as an adult for my crime, and asking the judge for a 15-30 year sentence.

It was highly probable because of the heinousness of the crime that I would get bound over and be sent to an adult prison earlier than I was supposed to. Time after time, I came to the realization that what I have done was very horrible and it affected me, society and the like. I went to court over and over. Some days, if not most, I didn't see the judge.

There was a staff who came to my cell to get me ready for court. The officers took me to court for the case that I picked up for five counts of assault where my friend was accused of stabbing an older man. He looked at my paperwork and asked, "Wow, you really been busy, huh?" He then proceeded to say, "I hope you didn't do what they say you did by stabbing that old lady but, if you did you deserve to go to hell." I knew that what he said came from a place of judgment and condemnation. Looking back, he was right.

At that time, there was a rap group from Boston called the Almighty RSO and they had a hit song, called "Hell Bound". It was a dark and eerie song like, Snoop Dog's

"Murder was the Case" that I mentioned earlier, but, a lot darker. The presence of hell was real in that song and even now, as I think about it. I guess I mention the song because I was hell bound and had no other way of explaining it.

Chapter Six
The Introduction

While I was incarcerated at a high security juvenile facility in Roslindale, Massachusetts called, the Judge J. Connelly Youth Center. There was a Bible study being offered to incarcerated youth and, to be honest, I was happy to be getting out of my cell.

I believed in God and was taught how to pray to Him as a kid. My parents would have my brother and I get on our knees at night and pray and, for a long time, that was the bedtime ritual. I never was an atheist in my views. I never felt that there wasn't a God, but He was the last thing on my mind for much of my deviant life.

The Bible studies were offered on Tuesday nights every week at 7 pm. When I first heard of the group being offered, I guess I thought it would be guys in suits and ties coming in to tell us how wrong the lifestyles we led were that led us to being locked up. Most of the kids there were from the violent city streets in Boston.

At the time, the murder count in Boston was in the hundreds per year. The men coming in were actually from these violent city streets. Some "stick up kids", drug dealers, gang bangers and the like. Some of them had been arrested for murder and have even acquitted receiving a second chance at life.

They looked different than I had imagined. They wore champion hoodies, jeans, timberland boots, had braids, fades and blowouts, and the name of the group was called, God's Posse. I have to admit I was mesmerized by the stories being delivered from shootouts, lives changed, acquitted cases and gang beef squashed.

It was like the posse existed at the right time and, during that time, blood was shed to a high degree in Boston. The police and the community couldn't stop the violence. God's Posse believed they were set up to stop it because of the fact that these same guys that ran the streets were the people were being body bagged. They had a message, a message of hope and inspiration for life change in a real and meaningful way.

I chose to get out of my cell. It was either that or stay stuck in there. What I did not know or realize was I was going to have an encounter with the Divine God that would stay with me for the rest of my life.

Most kids in there criticized those that picked up a Bible in lockup. We call it jailhouse religion and I didn't want to be one of those kids. So I attended for 10 months before I gave my life to Christ, believing in the message that Jesus died for my sins. I needed forgiveness. I spent many nights in my cell asking for it and I was attracted to the idea that my life could be salvaged and have a purpose, which is the message that God's Posse brought to us.

It got to the point where I looked forward to coming every Tuesday night and, not only did they teach us, but they also spent time with each of us in private, answering our world of questions, praying for our issues like our court cases, family, and the like.

I can remember this one guy in the group, named Nate. He told his story of being arrested for a murder he didn't commit at a party and spending a year in jail and hearing about how God spoke to him about his acquittal. He hypnotized us and had us on the edge of our seats. He very confidently and courageously told us about how he heard God tell him, "I, God, have the last word." What he said God meant by that was God had the last word on his life.

It was more than interesting hearing this because most of us would say to the group, how come God doesn't talk back? Looking back, I believe more than ever that God communicates with mankind. I think we are just not paying attention or ready to hear Him but, back then, his story sounded like something like an epic movie.

Little did I know, his story would be part of my decision to embrace Christ and, as a matter of fact, on a Tuesday night in 1995, this kid, who was a professing Latin king, and I would be led into a prayer of salvation by Nate, and my life would never be the same after that night. I embarked on a journey that would be lifelong and one thing about a journey or voyage is that they could be good or bad, but this journey has been thrilling, to say the least, and I don't regret taking that step that night.

Don't remember all that was going through my head that night, just that I didn't want to miss the opportunity and that I had waited 10 months and I had come to the point in my life that I realized it's one thing to make a mistake. It's a whole other thing to leave it uncorrected because of Street machismo and false ideals that hinder one's progress and leave one locked in a pattern. It is the machismo that makes one say you must keep it real with a lifestyle that's not going to keep it real with you.

In the streets, people are killed by best friends, testified against by fellow gang members, and are sent to prison where no one sends them canteen or bail money as promised. We were young, duped into believing that the streets were real, but the street names that people worshiped would be long gone and corrode by the time one would come home. I realized it was okay to correct my mistakes and that it was okay to embrace change while in prison.

Because I was sincere, I didn't really know or care too much about whether someone else was sincere, just as long as I knew I was. That's all that really mattered to me. So I accepted Jesus as my personal Lord and Savior on that Tuesday night in 1995 and, because I was real and knew I couldn't fool Him if I tried, it made me more sincere and real. I'm grateful for the opportunity that night brought into my life by the street soldiers, known as God's Posse that was formulated through the vision of a school teacher, named Rich, a man who was a Harvard and MIT graduate that didn't come from the wrong side of the tracks, but satisfied the need of inner city youth with the right heart. That heart helped me to save lives from the spirit of death that hovered and still hovers over Boston streets today.

I was introduced to God in a different way than I was introduced to my Catholic upbringing. I am not knocking on the devout followers of any particular religion who sincerely believe they have the answer or have benefited from the tenets of what they practice. However, I was introduced to Jesus, a Jesus that was in love with the rebel because he could see past the rebel's criminal history, devious and heinous acts, repeated failures and pattern of madness, and see that they need a rescue mission. God worked through the mission of God's Posse that believed in apprehending the rebels so that they might go out and apprehend other Rebel's that needed someone to go get them.

Sometimes, when you are running the streets, some people believe that there is no hope for you, and so they don't bother to offer hope to renegades, but even renegades and vigilantes need hope. If someone would dare to offer them hope, you will find that it has a ripple effect into the underworld that is positive and pushes back the spirit of death and brings life to those that are considered dead men walking.

Looking back, I was at the right place at the right time to hear from these soldiers. I think hear their stories, their ways and, it made me want to be a part of God's worldwide posse, a posse of former misfits, scoundrels, and criminals that had hope brought to them at some point and now bring hope to others on their respective levels, to the four corners of the Earth.

Chapter Seven
A General is born

It is important that one realizes that our identities are influential either in a negative way or a positive way. However, when one's life is transformed from bad to good, your wave of impact becomes more positive and far-reaching. I always wanted to be a professional basketball player. So, when I got locked facing 15-30 years and time as a juvenile in an adult facility, I quickly realized that I wasn't going to get a shot at playing basketball. The most basketball ball I was ever going to play was inside the gym in lockup.

I had hoped to remain in a juvenile facility, not because I accepted Christ, but because I was hoping that the courts would be more lenient on me, that I would be committed until I turned 21 and come home from the juvenile facility.

To be honest, thoughts of being in a state penitentiary scared me. It scared my peers too as they hear so many stories about prison rapes, stabbings, guys getting thrown off of tiers and prisons that have age old reputations for housing the worst of the worst and it taking a strong mind to make it out alive .

I was going back and forth to court for my bound over hearing to determine whether or not I would tried as an adult or a juvenile. My parents were there all the time to show the courts I had their support. Psychologists that interviewed me presented their reports to see whether or not someone like me with a case as heinous as mine could be responsible for this. After an 11 month hearing of what was supposed to be 6 months, the judge apologized to my family and said, "I'm sorry Mr and Mrs Belizaire, but we do not find your son amenable to treatment in a juvenile facility."

My parents were heartbroken and saddened. Looking back, they went through so much, missed days of work to be there for me, driving back and forth to lockup to make sure they saw me. They were going through bankruptcy and they were always finding a way to leave me money for what I needed. I hated to take money from them knowing their situation and knowing that I was putting them through the ringer by what I had done.

Looking back, it worked out anyway for me getting sent to an adult correctional facility because the five years I had gotten with an added 8 months of an 8-10 year prison sentence under the pre truth in sentencing law in Massachusetts, which stated that any one locked up before June/ July of 1994 would serve ⅔ of their sentence for a violent crime. Just that difference alone for me would have put me into adult corrections.

As I said before, I wanted to play ball. When I realized that I would be doing time, I desired something more for my life. I tried going to school but, instead, I got my G.E.D. That was a positive step in the right direction, but I was looking for something deeper, something more meaningful.

I remember there was this kid I knew from school who I used to play basketball with. I was reading about him in the Brockton Enterprise all the time while I was locked up. The phone was the only way to keep up with what's going on outside of the concrete and razor wire. He was breaking high school rushing records, having many scholastic achievements. I was so jealous.

I always envied him because there was this girl I had a crush on for so long and she liked him. I couldn't see why she didn't see me. Thinking about it now, I realized that it was puppy love and a phase. On a more serious note, I was jealous of what I read because it seemed like he had found a purpose in football. College scouts were looking at him and me, well, I had my dreams and potentials, but I was locked up. It's a tough thing when your dreams and potentials are caged. It's the worst feeling in the world. Simply put, it was the craziest frustration.

I remember going into my dark cell one night and praying to God to give me a purpose, praying for Him to give me something new because basketball was out of the window. Not too long after that, a Dominican kid on the unit, who was in for murder, got a Bible in the mail from his mother, a women of faith. The Bible was leather with gold pages. I remember seeing the Bible come in the mail during mail drop off on the unit.

Mail drop off on the unit was always an occasion of joy and sadness for some because some people got mail and some didn't. When they did, they were happy. Those who didn't just didn't bother to inquire because they knew that they had no one that would reach out to them through pen and paper. I occasionally got mail and, when I did, I felt like someone was thinking of me, like I was important and valued. It felt great to know that someone with a life in the free world would take time out of their busy schedules to jot me a few lines. I read the letters over and over again, meditating on every line and word, interpreting the meaning and feeling of things.

This kid got a Bible one day. I had seen the prison Bibles that were available to inmates and of them were tattered and torn, but this Bible caught my eye. I asked him if I could borrow it. He hadn't even looked at it yet, but he caved in because of my constant requests and let me borrow it for a few days. I devoured it like a madman.

I soon began to share what I was reading to my curious peers on the unit, inmates that were probably contemplating faith amongst many things while in their cells. I didn't know a lot, but they came to me with questions and I tried to answer them based on what I read. I got so much joy sharing with them, that I went to my cell one night and I prayed to God that I don't care if I have to spend the rest of my life in prison, just let me share you Word. When I started sharing the Bible with others, my soul would flood with joy, joy that brought a high that made me higher than any high I had ever experienced.

I was genuinely happy and the walls of prison didn't dictate my happiness. It was at that point that I discovered my purpose. Later in life, sometime after my release, I became a preacher. Looking back, it all made sense because the darkness I was enveloped in, the violence and people I associated with, the things I had seen made me into someone with something to say, and gave me the background of experience I needed to share with those who struggled or are struggled just like I did.

I started to run Bible study groups on the unit and in my cell. People called me Reverend, Pastor and Bishop. These were all terms of endearment for how I carried myself. This new identity allowed people to no longer see me by what I was in for, but someone who truly reflected what I wholeheartedly believed. Brothers wished me well and said that they knew, if I got out, I would keep it real with the God thing, unlike the many others who just had the jailhouse religions and the moment they beat their case or got bailed out, it was back to the life they swore they were done with and looked as if they did not skip a beat.

Anytime someone came on the unit that I knew or didn't know, I handed them a Bible and told them that I was studying and invited them to my study and they came. I spent the time to answer questions and pray with my brothers. I also gave them advice on their case, not from a jailhouse lawyer point of view, but from the standpoint of how they should go about it, in terms of whether or not they knew if they were innocent or guilty. The crazy thing about that was that most men in prison wouldn't tell you if they committed a crime, but some were so overwhelmed by deep guilt and confided in me. Some of them even wept in my arms.

I knew that this was what I was supposed to do, be a general, not be on the streets. I wasn't supposed to chase and idolize criminals, but let them know that there is forgiveness for them and a God that welcomed them, guilty stains and all. After all, he had welcomed me and I was just reassuring that what He did for me, He could do for them. God welcomes criminals too.

Chapter Eight
Masters, Mystics, and Mentors

It is important, that in anything, one has passion and is passion-focused. One should also find a master, mystic, or mentor that is operating in that very same passion in order for them to arrive at their end goal, which is to be like them and do what they do. Looking back, I've been extremely blessed to meet so many people that I can call a mentor.

Some would disagree and say that you should only have one mentor. I understand that logic and reasoning, however, each of my mentors operated in the same passion that I've been operating in. Each of them had both their strong and weak points.

Their areas of strength made me want to keep in touch with them, learn from them, and listen to them. I've also noticed their areas of weakness, not as a case for criticism, but as a basis for knowing who I can go to with certain things, who I can be helped by, and why I can or cannot be helped by certain people in any given set of circumstance.

While I was in prison, I met many men and women that cared for me during the 5 years and 8 months of my incarceration. Each of them were deeply flawed, but they were all sent or commissioned to reach the incarcerated deviant, the worst of the worst, the lost souls of society.

I've had the added blessing of still being in touch with most of them on some level 24 years after that fateful night the police surrounded my house and took me away, which as I've always said was a blessing because it kept me from the madness that was going on around that time. Many of my friends, peers, and associates had the spirit of death on them, which meant that some of them were getting shot, or shooting others. Some of them also got deep into drugs, which is another form of death in and of itself, selling death to the addicted on the streets.

I needed someone to guide me, to give me my desire to become a leader and a voice. The Lord brought me those people and, as a result, I have people to this day that I consider mentors on some level.

They are all doing different things these days and have experienced life on various levels, but one thing remains the same, their passion for helping others. I think when I was locked up, I needed others to walk with me, to help me through the days I was actualizing my faith in a real way. I had one mentor named Tim. I appreciated his deep insight on spiritual matters and I desired to have the same insight he had on things. He had an engineer's mind on spiritual things.

He was very good at breaking things down in an animated and real way. That was a strength that I would later develop and implement when helping others through my gifting and practice, lots of practice. I also had a mentor named Rich who I've mentioned earlier. I admired his spiritual maturity and his ability to care and take in criminals and disciple them to grow deeper and deeper in their journey. He was a math educator, so he was able to teach and teach well.

I also had a mentor named Mike who came alongside me after my incarceration, was faithful in being a point of contact, and whose counsel proved to be of immense value in critical times. I had a woman that became a second mother to me named Delia who spent decades of her life reaching the incarcerated knowing what it was like because she was a former prisoner herself and has a son in prison with a life term.

The list goes on and on of people that have impacted me. During and after lock up, I guess I needed a sense of direction regarding my purpose. I couldn't get it from my father because, although he loved me and was a great provider, he did not know his purpose, and one can only guide you in a way in which they know. I needed to learn how to respond to things because I was a hot head. Ever since I could remember, I would be fighting; always trying to prove myself, but the more I interacted and observed my mentors, the more I mimicked them, imitated them, and emulated their characteristics that I later found to be of great value in terms of the direction I was going in.

One thing that I learned was that, just because I was locked up and would be for a while, it did not mean that my life would be over. It did not mean that I couldn't be positive and help others around me. I interacted with people from various religious backgrounds, sometimes debating things and sometimes just having casual conversations. I hung around the older brothers in prison and they admired the maturity I had for being so young, which was accelerated because of my mentors and all the wisdom I was coming to know.

Even people from Muslim camps would politely call me Caliph, or Khalifa, which is the Muslim name that represents Allah on Earth. I was given the name by an ex-con who would observe me studying the Bible daily on my bunk bed, running groups, and teaching others what I was coming to know. I found that later in life, I would become a master, mystic, and mentor to others. It was a wonderful privilege to be able to make an imprint on the lives of others. It was because I had the privilege to have mentors that have devoted their time and effort to invest in my purpose, a purpose that I did not think could ever be possible.

Chapter Nine
To be a con, or not to be a con,
that is the question?

Sometimes our environments shape us, if not completely, then partially. We pick up the culture of the world that we know. The people in it and their conversations, mentality, philosophies, and principles affect what we personally say and do. I discovered that my purpose was to help those on the wrong side of the tracks in prison. It was not my whole purpose, but was part of it in that moment of time.

I knew that I would be locked up for some time and knew I had to grow accustom to being behind the razor wire. I ran into men in the county jail that were known as "true cons", which was those who spent 10 years or more behind the wall. They quickly tried me and my faith in God. A lot of their testing came from the standpoint of their worldview.

Some of them did multiple bids and carried the prison persona, and rightfully so because they deeply encompassed the harsh reality of jail / prison life.

I was in that world whether I wanted to be or not, so I often clashed with them because I was trying to incorporate my faith into the world I lived in. Needless to say, it was tough being a Christian in an environment that can be extremely hostile and volatile at any given moment. I often debated things with them and, with religion and such things, they held the view that Christianity was the white man's religion and was a way to brainwash and control the mind of the weak. I realized that I stood out because I was passionate and zealous in my faith. Also, my crime was big news so, needless to say, I was a notable inmate at the time.

I discovered that one does not have to surrender to one's environment, but can rise above it no matter how negative it is. There are some things that stay with me to this day even though I never embraced the con man mentality. One thing that is still with me to this day is the ability to be more aware of my surroundings. In jail or prison you need that desperately because there are always sneaky things going on. There are always fights, somebody getting ready to get jumped, receive a certain degree of burns, get hit over the head, or be stabbed.

Although I rose above the environment, there are some skills that I use even today that apply to dealing with people. However, I try not to choose to be ex-con in my mind even though I was surrounded by a bunch of them because my new found purpose told me I was so much more than that.

As a matter of fact, when I got upstate, the environment is intensified 10 times over the county jail. I remember I was in Concord

State Prison and there was a white man on my block (unit) that was serving life and waiting to go to Walpole MCI, Cedar Junction. He couldn't wait to go because he would be in a single cell and he could begin to serve his sentence with some peace. In prison, it's a luxury to have a cell to yourself. Who would've thought a lonely cell would be a luxury, but in the world of ex-cons and inmates, it is.

There was a growing tension between him and another prisoner. This prisoner was a black brother from Boston who shared a cell next door to him. I remember him being intimidating and massive. His eyes looked in different directions when he spoke to you, yet he was embraced by so many people. Anyhow, he was rapping on the block, a thing some inmates would do to pass time. Some of them would be in the yard flowing their latest raps and some would be on the unit. Well, this white man could not sleep because this brother stayed up doing this and, even though he was politely

One day, there seemed to be tension rising on the unit. Again, when one develops certain skills, you have more of an ability to just feel it sometimes. Out of nowhere, this white prisoner came with a lock in a sock and hits this the intimidating unit rapper over the head and busts his head wide open with blood everywhere.

The tensions were high and talk of a white prisoner vs. black prisoner beef was ensuing. I was operating as a Christian behind the razor wire and this was not a role I desired to play. This was my sincere faith lived out, but I could feel the tug of war within me debating whether or not I should be involved. It's funny how we can get signed up for things in the world we live in simply by association, whether in the ghetto, the street you're from, your job, or it may be those who want to strike vs. those who don't. For me, my skin color seemed to automatically volunteer me for this.

I ran into this white guy locked for a string of bank robberies and doing life. After he got out of the hole, we remembered each other from the county jail and he struck up a conversation with me and we spoke about the incident. I told him it wasn't worth a war. He looked at me and said, "You don't carry yourself like con and that's a compliment. Keep it up kid."

I think in his mind he had realized long ago that this con talk was foolishness, and that those who held on to it were only holding themselves back from progress. His compliment stayed with me even to this day. He was, by prison standards, considered a true con from Charlestown. He was known for doing time for legitimate crimes because he robbed banks. Yet, he complimented me on my demeanor and it made me realize that, in the world of lockup, you can either sink, let it suck you in, or rise above the environment.

I think of Malcolm X, who was in this very same prison I was at and, shortly into his bid, he discovered the greatness within himself. I guess your identity is what you want it to be. This idea is based on Proverbs 23:7, "Whatsoever a man thinketh in his heart, so he is". In my mind, I was determined to not let prison sink me. I had found a new identity and was going to live it out even behind razor wire and cement with a host of guards and hostile characters, for fellow inmates, and let the chips fall where they may because it was worth living out.

See, in lockup, you soon realize, after much time to think about how your path was self-destructive, you can either change or remain the same. If you change, you are more likely to reach the potential you have. If you remain the same, you will experience the adverse effects of that decision and it will have a significant impact on yourself and those who love you and want to see the best for you, such as your immediate family and friends.

Even though, as adults, we structure our lives around our independence, what we do for a living, and what we been through, we are still very much imprinted upon on a day to day basis. We must not allow our environments control our lives if it is going to have negative connotations in our lives.

The young man or woman from a violent or crime-ridden neighborhood doesn't have to partake in it but, instead, be the positive influence, even if they are standing alone. That influence carries a significant amount of weight in the world they live in. They are a light in the midst of the darkness. One match or candle burns bright in the dark and, if mine could still burn bright amongst murderers, armed robbers and the like, yours can too.

Although some would call me an ex con and, in theory, I am because I was convicted by the state, handed a sentence and served time in a Massachusetts penal system, I still never embraced it as my identity. My Walpole number was not my identity. My identity was and still is my faith in Jesus Christ.

There are a lot of labels that people will put on you and some you may put on yourself, but you've have to know what to accept and reject. Even today, I choose to reject the labels of my past and anything someone would try to put on me now that is not me. I think, just because I portray a certain image in someone's world, it doesn't mean that's who I am in my world.

The story of David and Goliath comes to mind. King Saul, the first king of Israel, tried to put military armor on the young David who was secretly anointed to take his place. David tried it, but could not operate in that anointing. He was supposed to go out in rags with rocks to defeat the 9 foot 9 inch tall Goliath. He didn't need polished armor. The story glorified him and his shepherd boy clothes because, after all, that's all he was. The training he received was not amongst the military elite. I've learned that you can't let people make you be who they want you to be. You just have to be yourself!

Chapter Ten
Muddy miracles

By no means does God acquit the guilty. Although, it seems like people get away with horrible things. What describes this point perfectly is the saying, "you might get bye but you can't get away " rings true. What I'm about to say is not some sort of testament to God condoning or turning blindly to what I did to go to prison, but it is a testament to the fact that He is merciful, extremely merciful.

During a period of time, I awaited trial for my case which was 3 years and 10 months. By this time, I was 19 years old. I was going back and forth to court and my court dates. It was a very exhausting time for me and my family. I can remember fellow inmates telling me that I was going to get "smoked", a term used for those that are punished to the highest degree for their crimes. I remember praying hard every day and night for God to have mercy on me.

I knew that I was guilty and I could not escape that because I was troubled by my conscious daily. I woke up every day and I was still in jail, I was hoping it all was just a bad dream but, every day that I woke up, I was still locked up and I had to face the harsh reality of what I had done to be there and how it derailed my life.

My attorney, which at the time was one of the most prolific attorneys they could have sent me, accumulated piles upon piles of court documents. It's funny how I ended up having him as a lawyer because my family had filed for bankruptcy and had no way of paying for decent legal representation for me. He kept in touch with me and sometimes he didn't, which added to my stress.

My attorney told me over and over about the severity of my case and that I most likely was going to do time, but he was trying to get me the least amount of time possible. Then it happened. After a lot of continued courts dates and talks with my family on the phone about my future, I went to court and two detectives from the Brockton Police Department had a hard time describing the color of the coat I was said I was wearing the night of the crime. One said it was brown the other said it was blue.

The judge was frustrated with the glaring discrepancies. I remember him calling the detectives color blind and ordering them to bring the jacket to the court house so that he could determine the color. Immediately, the court proceedings stopped and I was given another court date.

I remember asking the court officer how he thought it was going. I think I asked him that because all of the court officers in Superior Court had become well acquainted with me and my case. He said, "I don't know, but it's looking good for you." I went back to the county jail that I was an inmate in. A few days later, a prisoner communicated to me from a cell in another unit by showing me a newspaper in his cell window. It was my case on the cover of the paper, saying there was some missing evidence. Apparently, when the detectives went back to find the jacket, they could not find it and they didn't find my fingerprints on the knife or the purse. I was also never picked out of the photo lineup. They found out that there wasn't a body warrant issued for my arrest and that the clerk magistrate didn't remember issuing a warrant for my arrest.

It seemed like a beam of light on my case had shined from Heaven above. I remember one of my cellmates at the time said to me, "I don't know what God is doing, but he's up to something. You're lucky. God is imparting His mercy on you." It was an interesting time in my case.

I remember the judge had to make a decision as to whether the case should be dismissed or not. I was praying obviously that it would be. My lawyer's motion to dismiss was denied, but the evidence was suppressed because it was considered inadmissible in court. There were absolutely no talks of plea bargains until I began approaching trial.

I remember calling my mentor Tim from jail and asking him what I should do. He stated that I had to "soak this one in prayer", meaning I had to pray on it to decipher the best course of action. I did, but I still felt very conflicted. If I went to trial, there was the possibility of time, even though there was no evidence because there was still one witness who could put me in the area an hour before everything happened.

The others that were with me pleaded their Fifth Amendment rights and one of them was offered witness immunity to testify against me. He testified to my guilt, seeing everything from before, during, and after it happened. They offered me a 12-20 year plea bargain. I wrestled with it mainly because I wondered if my mom would still be alive when I got out. My lawyer came to visit me by surprise and said the district attorney was offering me 8-10 years.

At that time, I was talking to a lot of jailhouse lawyers who encouraged me to either go all the way or lower the time served, but I had become a changed man by this point. I knew that I was guilty and so I didn't want to think this was an opportunity to beat a case. So on March 19th, 1998, I plead guilty in Superior Court. The victim was in court at this time with her husband. I had the chance to see her for the first time face to face, I had the chance to testify to my guilt and my sorrow for what I had done.

I had the chance to testify about Jesus Christ and how he saved me. I was sentenced 8-10 years, of which I only had to do ⅔ of the sentence because it was a violent crime. This meant that I only had two years left to serve in the state penitentiary and I would be free.

To me, this was and is a muddy miracle, how God took a messy situation and redeemed it. Truth be told, I would still be there now if things swung the another way. I say all of this to say that God does not acquit the guilty, but he is certainly abundant in mercy.

Chapter Eleven
The devil hates goodbyes

Some say it's hard to say farewell to a relationship of any kind. The devil is real, an invisible, formidable foe of mankind. He loves to sink his claws into those that lives a life absent of God and, for a long time, that was me. I believed in a power beyond mortal man. I went to church as a kid, I prayed, but I was not saved, but when I finally decided to follow the pathway to Christ, I really felt the devil's grip on me and my mind. He wasn't taking my farewell to him easily.

I previously mentioned that I was in state prison named Old Colony Correctional Center. It was a level 5 prison, the only level 5 prison in Massachusetts, one step down from the notorious Massachusetts Correctional Institution (MCI) in Cedar Junction, Walpole. As a matter of fact, many men that were lifers who had obtained fewer infractions in Walpole ended up there. At the time, in 1999, Old Colony was an aggressive prison. It housed serious con men that were doing "screamers", which is a term used to describe an outrageous prison sentence. I recall that I was getting "short"(finishing up my sentence), and I was going to be released soon. I was in a cell on a unit where they placed troublemakers because I had verbally assaulted a prison guard who had stripped searched me for no reason in another facility.

Even though I had found redemption, I still had an edge to me. It is a necessity to have in prison. I was put in a cell with an older man that was just starting his bid. It was so tense that I could feel that, at any time, we were about to, what they call a "fair one", or one on one. We were toe to toe one night, but something came over me while were locked in that cell. It was an epiphany.

I realized I was going home and he was just starting out his sentence. If I hurt him bad enough, I could possibly lose the opportunity to have a good time with him if I hurt him, which would also delay my release date. I also realized that the devil didn't want to say goodbye to me, that he was losing a good foot soldier and that, at this critical time, he was influencing someone else that had less to lose to cause me to miss out on my blessings.

After that quick, but powerful moment, I said to the man I squared off with, "If you want to catch a rep off me and say you checked me, you got that." He denied that he wanted that. I was later moved into another cell on the same unit with a lifer that liked the way I carried myself as a young man and we had many good conversations about my future, and the most powerful thing he said to me was, "I did a 3-5, wrapped up, and went home. I wasn't out there long, and now I'm doing life. You got a chance that I won't have. Don't mess it up and, if I see you back in here, I'm beating you down." It was really a way of saying, "Don't come back here because you have a chance that I don't. I got love for you man."

Matthew 12:43-45 says, "When an impure spirit comes out of a person, it goes through arid places seeking rest and does not find it. Then it says, "I will return to the house I left." When it arrives, it finds the house unoccupied, swept clean and our in order. Then it goes and takes with it seven other spirits more wicked than itself, and they go in and live there. And the final condition of that person is worse than the first. This is how it will be with this wicked generation". (NIV)

I say that to say this, since my release was coming soon, I was concerned about the transition into the free world. I wanted to never go back to prison. I wanted to carry my new found faith as a free man and live changed. In prison, so many people talk religion, but quickly forget the faith they profess. As a matter of fact, it's a source of discouragement to those who are sincerely inquiring to learn more about their faith and make the necessary changes in their life. It's a discouragement for others.

I often told fellow prisoners that it is a misrepresentation of God and, the problem is not God, but the men themselves. So, despite the counterfeit life they were living, it didn't stop me from being a genuine representation of God. I wanted to be free following God, which resulted in an opportunity to go live at the God's Posse Residential Program. I wasn't mandated to go, but I chose to go in an effort to be successful in my goals. After nearly 6 years of not being home, my parents did not understand why I wanted to go into a program. It didn't last too long because I only spent about a month and a half there before I went home on a pass.

During my first day back in Brockton, I smoked weed, drank and went to a party where there were beautiful women. Immediately, this life became more enticing because I have been locked up at a very young age and for a long time. I never went to a club and didn't really have a girlfriend. I missed out on getting my driver's license, prom, etc. The excitement of the world kicked in. The devil didn't want to say goodbye; that invisible force that manifests itself in the immorality of men did not want to let me go.

I started a fight with one of the managers of the program after demanding I get a key to the house, so my cousin came pick me up in the middle of a blizzard. I had walked out of prison with my right-hand man. He has been my best friend during those years behind the razor wire. My mentor Tim had accompanied my parents to pick me up from prison to the program situated in Boston. He said that after all the years of supporting me, he would be there to witness me coming home, and now, I was leaving the program to dance with the world. I said that I didn't want to be a part of it.

They say the road to hell is paved with the best of intentions. I definitely had good intentions, but was quickly deviating from them. Surprisingly, when I returned home, unbeknownst to me, my parents were renting to people that were weed abusers, cocaine users, and alcoholics. On my first night back, there was a knock on the door. It was a friend from many moons ago. I got excited when I opened the door. He put his index fingers over his lips, told me to hush and come upstairs.

I was greeted by people that I didn't know. They told me that they had heard of me and were happy to meet me. They asked me what I wanted to drink and told me they would buy. They were smoking weed and I joined them. Apparently, the guy renting from my parents was an uncle to the kid who came to the door looking for me. I don't think my parents realized all that was going on with the people they were renting to, until later. Unfortunately, it became like another prison for me.

Whenever I tried to get on the straight and narrow, I felt pulled in the direction of that apartment. I was out of a job for two years after my release, so I had way too much time on your hands. When you have too much time on your hands, you tend to be unproductive and life becomes wildly unmanageable because you have no sense of direction. So, I wavered back and forth between alcohol and drugs and my faith and was just trying to do all the right things.

Finally, I found success and, for the last two years of them renting from my parents, I did not go upstairs. I didn't want to be anti-social. I just wanted to be free and sometimes, to be free, one must have an element of antisocial behavior because some company is not worth keeping if you desire to reach your destiny.

Chapter Twelve
The Marvelous Mission

A mission is basically an assignment, one that is serious and meaningful to those who are the beneficiaries of that mission and who are sent to fulfill it. I recall one day randomly asking a young teenager that I knew from my neighborhood to study the Bible with me.

I asked him because he seemed open to spiritual things and also because he was living with a foster parent He was frequently up to mischief and was experimenting with drugs, like marijuana and alcohol, and had way too much time on his hands to get into trouble.

Surprisingly, he said yes. I guess I was surprised because, in my experience, most people have a bone to pick with God and the stories and teachings of the Bible because they are counter the ways of society. Most people struggle with having faith in a God that they cannot see that allows so much pain in this world, and with a book that many have said has been tampered with and has no relevance to today's world.

These are things I don't fully agree with. This kid and I had a Bible study and a fire was ignited both in me and in people that I asked to study with me. Sometimes I did not know what to talk about, but when I did, it was always brief. Interestingly, one thing I did notice was that the people wanted more.

I knew I was making an impact when this kid Will contacted me while I was at work. I was surprised to get a phone call from him at my job. I thought it was an emergency with my family. Instead, it was him calling me sobbing, telling me how he wanted to change his life and was so thankful that God had sent me into his life to teach him the Bible.

I guess, if one wants to be part of a mission, you have to jump into that stream and let the stream carry you wherever it goes. Besides my one on one Bible studies with folks, I was going into the Department of Youth Services reaching out to kids that were at risk or proven risk and they responded well to me. They called me down to earth and said they love the way I broke down the Bible for them.

I got so much joy walking to the lockup and back home every day. It didn't matter the day or the weather and, even though I didn't have a car, I made it there 5 days a week and visited about 30 teens a week for a half hour with each kid and I saw so much proof of the divine. I was really seeing what I was doing was good and was impacting lives.

I also began to write letters to men in the county, state, and federal prisons. Every day, I got two to three pieces of mail and sometimes more from men that were either doing significant time or life in prison. You see, it's hard to be in prison and, when you feel forgotten by family and friends, it only adds to the pain. I know this first hand. Having been a former prisoner, I can't tell you how much joy I got when I finished writing a letter sent it off. I didn't believe in waiting to send letters either. I just went to the mailbox and it did not matter what time of the night it was.

I also realized the power of using one's own money to fuel the mission. I believe money is energy and it energizes one's plan and vision so I started using the money I had to pay to receive collect calls from those in prison, and to take people out to eat and talk about God over a good meal. I began to send money out to those in prison so that they could have a canteen and necessary items. I supported the men in prison for about ten years and volunteered at the juvenile hall for 6 years.

Meanwhile, my experience was being stretched and developed. I not only did prison ministry, but I was involved in so many other things as well that built my mental fortitude and shaped me in the process that would prove to be useful down the road as a pastor.

On that note, when most young men become involved in full-time ministry, they are rather green and wet behind the ears (tell me what this means). They may have seminary education, but they lack the practical experience to navigate the new waters they are chartering in so, of course, they have to make many mistakes and blunders before they can gain ground.

I would later become a pastor, a life long dream and ambition. I noticed that, when I got there, I shined brighter because I took on the missions that were less admirable and it made me better because of it. I think each of us have a mission. The question is, what do we do about the need that is right in front of you? Do we stand around idle or do we ask God if we should embark and, if he says yes, will we go? This is important because, in the end, your life becomes richer as you try to enrich the lives of others.

The mission of our life can produce marvelous results because we will marvel at how we will be used to meet the desperate needs of others and the need to recognize for ourselves that we have meaning and purpose. One does not have to be in a church, temple, synagogue, mosque, or some holy and sacred sight to find meaning.

I believe sanctified places are wherever the divine is and, wherever the divine is, there is sacredness. Since he is also everywhere at the same time, there is no place, absolutely no place that one cannot find the divine power that has set the world into motion with the intention of adding a mind blowing experience that can only be found in being in alignment with Him and his laws.

Chapter Thirteen
From the gutter to the palace

There is no doubt in my mind that experiences shape our perspective, our understanding, our choices and the way we make our choices. They shape what we like and dislike, our associations and the culture that comes with those associations and, as a result, it adds different levels of richness that a culture brings.

I mentioned in an earlier chapter how my mission and my various ministerial experiences gave me the practical tools for reaching out to those in the gutters of life, but now I want to talk about how the gutters shaped me as a person. We all hit low points in life. These include times of perpetual darkness, setbacks, frustrations and times of being lonely and saddened either because of the choices we made or the choices of others.

I became a pastor in 2013. Prior to that, I had been preaching for 7 years, traveling within the preaching circuit. It all started in October of 2006 when I preached my first sermon, "All that Glitters isn't Gold". By 2011, I was working as a community organizer in Brockton, MA. I was the first black organizer from Brockton. Most of the organizers had come to the city, but few actually stayed long enough to have any real influence on the people in the city and the work that needed to be done. That was why there was such a high turnover rate of employees.

I had high hopes coming in, but soon sensed that maybe I wasn't meant to be an organizer long-term, but just gain the experience. I got fired from the job because I wasn't a good fit for the role. I was encouraged more to pastor. I became a pastor about a year and some months later. So many people were at my installation services; but even though I preached my heart out for 3 years I ended up not staying and resigning to irreconcilable differences with my staff.

After that, I did work in a detox for 5 years. I saw people who were truly in a gutter situation. I always felt that the detox was my church because I helped so many people and so many people helped me to understand the being we call God so much better.

As a result, I came to see that, in order to know change and a true manifestation of identity, you have to understand that sometimes the gutter will have to shape you. There is something about rising from the gutter that makes you fit for life, adds meaning and real substance to your life.

It makes you deeper as a person. As humans, we tend to have our own plan, but

God has His own. Sometimes that plan is to go through the gutters in order to understand the meaning of life more and be able to identify with those who are currently in a gutter-like situation. To be honest, one can't metaphorically live in a palace unless they are living in a palace in your mind. On that same note, the gutter is also a mental state of being that we find ourselves in and, sometimes, if not most times, it's hard to make it out, but where one has the will to live past one's troubles, a person also has the ability to will themselves out.

I once heard the story of a dog that was stuck in a Czechoslovakian gutter. The rescuers came to get him and provide help. They said that they could smell the stench of death on this dog and that he was dying and maggots began to grow on him.

Although he was in very bad shape, they noticed that he still had the will to live because of how he was able to feebly make his way towards the rescuers even though he had no strength and was severely malnourished. See, the dog possessed the determination to make it out of his situation. I tell this story to people very often and let them know to not let a dying dog possess more will to live than you because the human will has extraordinary capabilities.

I've heard stories of women having her baby trapped underneath a car, and that woman, with a 5 foot 3 frame would pick up the car and get her baby out. The cry of her child was motivation enough to not let the car become an obstacle.

This brings to mind a gutter that I was in years ago. I had a nervous breakdown and mentally I was going through so much. It was during a time in my life that I was 2 years without a job because of my criminal record, I was abusing heavy amounts of potent marijuana and drinking alcohol periodically.

I was struggling to keep my faith active by reading my Bible as much as I could, listening to music that was spiritual and harness what seemed to escape me at the time, which was a stable life. I finally broke down after trying to keep it together for so long. I was in a gutter and ended up becoming hospitalized.

I did not know what the future held for me, but I remember while being on a psychiatric unit in Brockton Hospital seeing a copy of a Sports Illustrated. It was during the time of what the NCAA called, "March Madness" and, on the cover, it showed some athletes and the word, "survivor". I cut those words out and pasted them on a piece of paper with a prayer I had written. I kept telling myself that I would survive. Sometimes you have to talk to yourself about your gutter situation in order to make it out. That is what I did and, by the grace of God, I made it out.

Talking to yourself is the same as talking to your subconscious. Although you are very conscious that you are in a gutter, your subconscious will tell you that you will not stay there. It seems foolish to some people to speak positively about oneself when the world is falling apart around them, but words have power and, by speaking to yourself, you are counseling your soul and telling your soul that you will not be defeated in any way.

King David says in Psalm 43:5, "Why, my soul, are you downcast? Why so disturbed within me? Put your hope in God, for I will yet praise him, my Savior and my God." King David went through perpetual trouble and learned to coach his soul by speaking to his subconscious and acknowledging his inner self through turmoil. This is one of the ways that one makes it out of the gutter and into the palace. Gutters are never pleasant but, even in the gutters, you become messengers with a message that says, despite all of the difficulty you will face, you can still make it to the palace.

Chapter Fourteen
Spirituality, Life and People

Before I entered into my positive identity, there were some barriers that had to be broken in my mind such as, the limitations and deficiencies that, as a result, hindered my abilities. Prior to prison, I was outgoing and a friend to many. However, when I was in prison, I became antisocial. It's not that I was a negative person. It's just that, in prison, you only hang with a select few, eat with a select few at the chow hall and walk the prison yard with the same people and usually all those people look like you, talk like you and think like you.

So when I came home, I wanted to meet new people. I wanted to be social and fun to be around, but I would freeze up every time I had to make conversation with someone new. Sometimes I turned to alcohol and marijuana, yes alcohol and marijuana, to feel social and, even though I was enhancing my capacity to be social through mind-altering and mood-altering drugs, I still was at a loss for words.

Sometimes our antisocial behaviors are learned and programmed into your day and behavior and, after spending 5 years and 8 months in prison, I was programmed to operate a certain way. Some people call it being institutionalized. I didn't miss prison like some who've done long stints of it. I didn't eat the same prison meals like some do when they leave prison, but I did carry with me a behavior of keeping to myself and being more introverted that made my dreams of working with people more difficult.

When I told people my troubles, they asked, "Why? You have such a beautiful personality." So, I prayed on it and, gradually, I began to break out of the antisocial behavior that hindered me from meeting and enjoying the company of new people.

Sometimes, in certain forums and events, it attempts to creep up, but I learned that people are people wherever you go, and I have been fortunate enough to meet people with some pretty unique life experiences that have made my existence and human experience powerful, which has help me to interact with all colors, cultures, beliefs, educational backgrounds, financial status, and conditions. This has shaped my personality and spiritual self in a positive way and has made me more down to earth.

It's funny that people are antisocial in church. They only associate with a particular clique. People in mosques sometimes only associate with those that go to mosques, people in temples only with those that go to temples, people in business with those that are in business, people in education with those that are in education, people in politics with those that are in politics, etc. When one has prejudices, biases, preconceived notions, or a racist heart, they rob ourselves of the blessing of the human experience that God has intended.

Proverbs 18:24 says "A man that has friends must show himself friendly, but there is a friend that sticks closer than a brother." and I've found friends over the years that have proven that blood is not always thicker than water.

I say all that to say, if you are going to have a quality identity, it will be shaped by the experiences you either allow or not allow yourself to have. Therefore, we must be saturated by others to be part of the human experience the Lord has intended for us.

Chapter Fifteen
Deep seas, Weeds, and Ocean floors

The Bible talks about the prophet Jonah and his rebellion and how he was casted into the sea wrapped in weeds and entrenched in the guts of a whale. Needless to say, he was in a very deep and dark place. Prison, for me, was the equivalent of that. As a matter of fact, some of the prisoners commonly called being in prison "the belly of the beast". It's interesting how deep and dark places bring enlightenment. You are probably wondering how a dark place could have the potential to bring light.

Part of the reason is because darkness reminds us of our frailty and our desperation. One does not have to go to prison to be in a dark place. We all, at some point in our lives, find ourselves in a dark place, and sometimes it is a divine order that we ended up there because we forgot what is essential in life.

Please, notice that I did not use plurality when I said essentially because sometimes what we think is essential is not essential, but God is an essential sometimes in our waywardness, we get a bad case of amnesia and we forget that we have a moral obligation to a Creator.

We forget that we are accountable to a higher order and sometimes we need a bad circumstance to change our hearts. Some people say that, when one is in prison, they are very humble. They realize the importance of family, friends, the choices they make, and the need for change. It's almost like darkness awakens them to the ever-present reality of the divine God.

I'm thankful that I got locked up. I sometimes wonder, if I hadn't where my life would have ended up. So many people I know were shot or killed while I was doing time and became addicts, never reversing the curse of addictions on their life.

Some people were trapped in a perpetual state of misfortune. It's not your darkness alone that enlightens one's life, but also how one responds to it. Some people settle for it, grow comfortable in it and there are some that do not even fear it, but some people are shaken by it and they are shaken into remembrance of God.

Maybe they learned about God from church, a praying grandmother or maybe they had a belief or persuasion that a God existed. I always believed that God existed. I just did not serve him or had any commitment to Him. The Bible mentions that once Jonah remembered that God, amongst the deep seas, weeds and ocean floors, spoke to the fish and the whale vomited him out. It seems almost cruel of God to do such a thing, but sometimes God will take drastic measures when other measures are not working. It is His loving reminder that we need Him and, in order to need him, you have to be in a circumstance that communicates that you do.

I'm not saying that God made me commit a crime to be in the belly of prison, but He did allow it so, in the end, I would remember him. Some say better to have loved than to not love at all or better to have lived than to not live at all.

God says it's better to remember than to not remember at all! Memory is a gift, a token of important information, information that is vital to one's life and existence and, when I remembered my Creator, He spoke to the belly I was in and delivered me.

However, He will only speak when there is a positive response to the deep seas, weeds, and ocean floors we find ourselves in. As long as we are reluctant to respond accordingly, we will be tormented by a dark place.

God is not egotistical in his wanting us to remember him, but it is like someone traveling on a plane and forgetting the emergency instructions. One needs those instructions in order to survive. Not everyone remembers, but for those that do, they are sure glad that their memory was jarred and that they were called to remembrance the God beyond the cosmos, and Creator of it, before it was too late.

I've talked to so many people who ignored God and who mocked their need for Him but, in the most humbling of times, a light bulb went off, and they said, "Aha! I know what I need to do. I need to call on God."

However, for those that are too prideful, haughty, and conceited, they only remember what cannot help, which are vain idols that will not suffice, especially when one is in deep and dark places. God will always be the One to show us that these temporary things will never compare to what He deems necessary.

Chapter Sixteen
Creating Significant Distance

One thing that has contributed to a real and live change in my life was the distance created between who I was and who I am today. When I first began to sense change in my life and profess change in my life, I could not, at times, accept the fact that others did not readily agree with my change.

The reason was not that people did not believe that change for someone like me was possible. It was that there was enough distance between my previous, selfish, and deviant identity to the identity of a loving and warm person who helps others to reach their full potential and human relevance. One of the things that were crucial and relevant for me was that I let time do its work on the hearts and minds of others as I moved in the direction that I wanted to.

The people who mentored me taught me that, over time, people would see my progress without me having to announce it and come to trust me and see that I was sincere. I mentioned earlier that I worked with those caught in the grips of addictions, and one of the hardest things for them, and it sometimes leads to relapse, is people not accepting, applauding, and approving the changes that are significant to them, but them being held in caution and speculation by others.?

.

I remember the story of a young woman who acquired 6 months of sobriety from a life of a ravaging heroin addiction. She came home to her mother, and hoped her she would be happy that she had been clean for this long. Unfortunately, she did not get the response she wanted and her mother replied with disregard and skepticism.

Now for an addict it's hard to get one day clean, let alone 6 months, but for her mother needed more proof and time. However, because this young woman didn't realize that there must be significant distance between who you once were and who you are now. Unfortunately, she relapsed due to the discouragement and never acquired that significant time of sobriety again.

I remember being in prison and announcing my change to my parents over the phone. They were very pleased to hear that I was making strides to change. After all, they had hoped and prayed for this to happen.

They always told me the real test is continuing on as a changed man when I left prison, and this thought and statement was true, but it also hinted that they needed more time to come to a place to truly be able to say that their son was a changed man, though I was sincere about my change.

I needed more time to be certain that I was going to stay in the direction of change as well. Distance not only verifies change, but it gives you milestones to look back on and, the more milestones you have, the more markers there are of accomplishments and success. These makers and milestones serve as encouraging reminders of who we once were and who they are now becoming.

Chapter Seventeen
Unfinished business

There is an immense danger and tragedy in leaving things incomplete. Some people are satisfied with attempts and halfway achievements, but one must learn to follow through in what they start in order to be successful at what they do.

I think of the world renowned pitcher Nolan Ryan. He was an excellent pitcher, a threat on the mound to any batter. One of the things that made Nolan Ryan so great was, not just being able to throw the ball at high speeds of velocity, but he can also follow through with his pitches and get the ball into the catcher's mitt.

See, in the end, everything is about follow through. I've learned and am still learning that 99.9% is never good enough when it comes to goals and ambitions. I'm not saying that I've completed everything I've attempted, but I still see the value in finishing things versus not finishing.

I remember being in prison and feeling that I was a changed man, but I had to address loose ends with people that I offended in some way. One of the greatest requests for forgiveness was addressed to the victim in my case when I came to court on March 19th, 1998 to plead guilty to my charges. I had thought about it prior because I knew she would be there and my attorney told me I would have a chance to address the courtroom. I remember thanking my Lord and Savior Jesus Christ for the sentence that was about to come forth and I remember turning around to address the victim and her husband and ask for forgiveness for what I had done.

I knew that my sentence was my sentence and that, as far as the court was concerned, there was no more continued court dates, paperwork and the looming concern and stress of what my future would be. However, there was unfinished business in terms of addressing her. She did not comment on what I said, but she listened. She gave a victim impact statement that was very gracious from what I recall.

Although I did not get a response from her, I was able to complete that part of my life in the best way the circumstances allowed. If I had not taken advantage of the courtroom that day to address her, I would have lived in regret forever. This is the reason that one should take care of loose ends, unfinished business, and then follow through.

Chapter Eighteen
Juggernauts and Kings

The term "juggernaut" is a term that was created by the belief that the Hindu god, Vishnu incarnated himself as "juggernaut" or "jagganatha". A temple was erected to this god and many festivals are held during the year in honor of juggernaut and, during the year, a 60 foot image is paraded through the streets and some devout worshipers offer themselves as sacrifices by allowing themselves to be crushed under this image as worshipers rejoice in a celebration of it.

Hence, juggernaut refers to dealing with an unmatched and destructible force, and the term "king" has to do with a sovereign power of the nobility. This force is a male and is supreme in his ways. In order to operate on a higher plane, one must be like a juggernaut and like a king, but one does not wake up and become this. It is a process that starts with one's thinking, and then leads to one's habits, then one's associations and finally the results.

I've been blessed in my life to be around these type of individuals that embody the qualities and are devoted to what the juggernaut represents. The interesting thing is how they think. Small-minded people think and behave as such because they have been conditioned to do so.

I remember when I noticed that the numbers on my cell phone were of people that were positive and thought the way that I was thinking or was similarly looking to elevate their thought patterns. The saying, "Birds of a feather, flock together" is true. One does not become great overnight, but with ongoing dedication, one has a greater ability to arrive at that point. I had to learn not to be content with where I was at as a person. Contentment is a virtue, but it's not productive to be content with mediocrity and being average. It all starts with the mind. Reading books helps to cultivate the juggernaut in you and the vast experiences of life if you choose to learn from them what you need to do to be better. If you do not have access to people personally, then books can be your best friends, books that carry a positive message and create versatility in a person to be able to communicate to others on their level.

Some characters I enjoyed reading about were Nelson Mandela and Haile Selassie, learning about how they moved, operated, and impacted, at times, the way I viewed and approached circumstances. Books not only are the best mentors, but they improve one's cognition and feed the mind of the reader. The mind is like a sponge and we exude what we absorb and absorb what we release in our thoughts, speech, and behavior.

Chapter Nineteen
Naysayers of Change

I spoke earlier about creating distance as you are in the process of changing by allowing people and yourself the time to establish a proven track record of change. However, there are some people that, no matter what you do to correct past mistakes, improve your lifestyle and quality of living, will always be enemies of your change and will refuse to accept that you've changed despite the overwhelming proof that something special has occurred in your life.

The one thing you must not do is waste time trying to convince others that are determined to not be convinced of your change. Naysayers can include, family members, friends, people in society, coworkers, religious persons, and the like. I believe that, sometimes, in the spiritual realm, certain people are used by dark forces to discourage and discontinue your progress.

The fact that people are opposed to your change shows that what you are doing has come to their attention but, because they are operating in negativity, they will still refuse to accept that change. I recall an occasion where I was mentoring some young men on a weekly basis. We had such a powerful and enjoyable time. We would go out to eat and discuss an array of subjects. Our opinions fed one another spiritually and in other ways as well.

However, there was a friend of one of the guys who attended our weekly meetings and she said that she knew me, my past and what I was all about and claimed that I was practicing nothing but jailhouse religion. I was taken back by her comments as I felt I had come a long way in my progress. I was working, driving a car, and been reaching out to others such as, at-risk and proven-risk youth. I was not doing the things I used to do and associating with the people I used to, yet she did not believe I had changed. Her words had a negative effect on one particular young man in my group. I felt that way because the of questions he would ask me and how often he brought up what she said.

I realized that what's more important, isn't what the naysayers say about your change, but how you handle their denial and disapproval of your change. Although words have power and can negatively impact others if not guided by a positive spirit and positive thinking, one must still think of the bigger picture when dealing with the naysayers. The bigger picture is ultimately what you are striving for and what you are after.

Naysayers are usually negative people that have poor self-esteem and whose lives are not going after change. Even the fact that they go out of their way to discourage, frustrate, and defeat you by calling out your past, is a sure sign that you are important, relevant and are making impact in a special way.

The best thing to do is keep your response short and tactfully positive. That way you do not lose what you are trying to achieve by paying attention to those whose words reflect their character and position in life. Naysayers have been around since the beginning of time and will be until the end. The goal is not to get rid of them, but to learn to pursue your heartfelt goals while still living with them, whatever their relation or association may be to you.

Sometimes, we can learn from them and, although what they say is fueled by negative energy, we still become wiser in learning how to deal with them and keeping sight of the bigger picture at hand. This has allowed me and has given me the ability to be able to continue to mentor these young men until they did not need me anymore.

I sometimes wonder if those who denied and refused my change would have been given more power if I had chosen to fight or argue with them. Fortunately, I did not argue with them or even give them the satisfaction of an argument. I have pressed on and continue to press on towards my change.

Chapter Twenty
Summoning Ghosts

When I was incarcerated, there was a point where things were looking pretty good for me, case wise. I remember coming back to the jail I was housed in with good news. Inmates quickly came to me to ask me how everything went.

I told them that I remembered going to the phone because the phone were "blazing". Blazing was a term that was used by inmates when blocked numbers were able to be called. Sometimes, those that have certain blocked numbers cannot receive a call from the county jail, and there are times where something would happen with the phone systems and they all were able to go through.

This was one of those days, so everyone was on the phone or trying to get a turn on the phone. I was tempted to call some old friends from the streets to fill them in on my progress with the courts. At the same time, I felt a strong urge not to call them.

I always had a love for my friends from the streets, but it had been years since I was inside. I basically grew up in prison all of my teenage years and that was my own doing, the bed that I made. I did not feel a real connection with people from my past anymore the years inside prison walls had evaporated that.

At that time, I realized that part of living out my new positive identity was disconnecting from old friends that were not traveling on the new path that I was on. This was difficult because it seemed like I was being disloyal to them, like I lacked solidarity and thought that I was better than them because I had a newfound religion and God in my life.

The truth of the matter was that I was summoning ghosts. To summon a ghost basically means to try to reach back and connect with people that have been out of your life. They were in your life at one point in time when you were thinking, feeling, talking and behaving a certain kind of way.

However, it was the past and, sometimes, we relive the past through old connections, and soon find out that the connection does not contribute positively to your new way of life. Many people fall into this trap. It is not that they are not changed or are insincere about changing but, metaphorically speaking, they have conducted a séance and they are reconnected with the ghost of the past. The danger with that is that it will haunt their newfound dreams and maybe even stop them indefinitely.

We love the past, old songs, old hairstyles and clothing that go out and then come back in style. We reminisce on old tales as if they are brand new. We talk about how life used to be. However, if we are going to disconnect ourselves from the ghosts in our life, we have to realize that there is a new glory. It is out with the people, places and things that brought us that strong nostalgic feeling, and in with the new.

We, as people, are always being shaped and reshaped by the moments, experiences, people that we meet, etc. In order to say hello to the new self, we must be able to part ways with the old because sometimes, calling on the ghost will take the life out of one's dreams and make them a ghost as well. Just a thing that once was alive , and no longer is because someone from your past has killed your dreams.?

After I learned that I could live without the friends from my past, life gave me new friends that complimented my newfound lifestyles and goals. I found that I was surrounded by fellow dreamers, people with ambition, and a good idea of the direction they were going in. Once you begin to see that in your life, you then will know that you have ceased to summon the ghosts and you will start to operate in the land of the living.

Chapter Twenty-One
Ill-gotten Gain

The term ill-gotten gain happens when what one acquires is done through a dishonest and wicked manner. I earned a reputation amongst my peers for doing so. As mentioned before, my friends called me "sticky", short for sticky fingers. There was a rap artist by the name of Sticky Fingaz, where I got my nickname, from the rap group "Onyx", a popular hip hop group that portrayed the male as angry with a hyped up bravado. This mainly represented their style. The lead artist, Sticky Fingaz speaks emphatically in one song called, "Throw Ya Gunz". Some of the lyrics included, *I'm a bald head with a knife. I want your money or life*.

It's interesting how nicknames describe a certain persona and how we do our very best to live up to the name we have acquired, and such was the case with myself. This persona caused me to pursue ill-gotten gain and the like. It set the pathway for my thoughts, my words, my behaviors, and habits, but something happened when I discovered that being "sticky" is what led me to facing the rest of my life in prison. I realized that I didn't want what the persona and the craving for ill-gotten gain gave me I was sitting in a cell at night overwhelmed, stressed, and having suicidal ideations.

I realized that most of my peers were locked up because of things that were acquired in an evil way and they all echoed the same thing and said, "It wasn't worth it." I say all this to say that some may not go to an extreme like I did for Ill-gotten gain but, anytime we acquire things through dishonest methods, we pay a price. I began to understand more in jail that drug dealing was foolish because, all though the money was fast and in abundance, the price one pays for that immediate gratification, is immense.

It's better to earn an honest check to keep a sense of dignity and pride because it is better to know that is was acquired legally and legitimately, than to suffer the shame of poisoning someone's mother or father, daughter or son for the Almighty dollar. I live now a life that's legit and I know I've earned what I own. When I look around the place that I live and everything I have I worked hard for, it's a testament to the change that has occurred in my life.

There was a time when I was "sticky", the young deviant that felt he had to steal, deceive, and rob his way to a comfortable living. Now sticky is no longer who I am, and a new person has come alive. Ill-gotten gain is no longer an attraction, nor an option for me. It is a fool's passion, but a wise man or a wise woman knows the satisfaction and joy of earning what they keep.

Chapter Twenty-Two
Motivated to move mountains

Part of my journey was learning the power of motivation. My definition of motivation is to be carried by a wind of inspiration towards an end that is desired and is positive. Right now, motivational speaking is a big thing because of the immense rewards it brings monetarily to those who have an awe-inspiring story or who have the natural or divine gifting to motivate others towards their life's vision and dreams.

Throughout my journey, I've faced many obstacles, which I will call mountains and, sometimes, these mountains are fairly sizable and, sometimes, they are enormous, daunting and fierce. The temptations that I faced with these mountains in my life is to just sit there and gaze at them and say there is no way that I could move past the mountain. However, motivation has been the key element that has helped me move the mountains in my life.

Sometimes the motivation came from hearing a message from a speaker, and sometimes it came from an inspirational songs, from recognizing my life purpose, from someone telling me how much I helped them, from a scene in a movie and sometimes it came from a phone call.

However, most times it came from, what I call, my inner fire. It was me pushing me past the obstacles. I've had so many in my life. Some people have said that I've been through so much as a young man and, when I heard it said to me, it sounded far-fetched, but sometimes you go through so much and you don't realize it, and sometimes God caused you to forget what you been through by giving you an overwhelming blessing that outweighs the struggle on the way to the blessings.

The Hebrew name for Joseph means, "to increase", and his Egyptian name means, "revealer of secrets". Joseph had two sons, Manasseh which means, "The Lord has caused me to forget my troubles" and Ephraim which means, "The Lord has made me increase in the land of my suffering". Joseph went through a lot as a young man. He was hated by family, persecuted for his visions, falsely accused of his righteous stance but, with all the mountains in

Joseph's life, I believe he learned the secret of personally motivating himself in God, what God told him, and what he hoped for. Even though he went through hell, his hell became Heaven because of God's redemption and because he stayed motivated.

This is something that a seasoned person knows how to do. As you learn to do this, the mountains in life decrease in size because they are not as big as your motivation! By no means am I perfect at this, but I have learned through much practice to stay motivated even when it seems that your motivation will not achieve much for you.

I recall hearing the story of former NFL player, Robert Conrad, who swam 9 miles to shore after a boating incident. It took 10 hours to swim to shore, and studies that one develops hyperthermia after three hours in deep and dark cold waters. He was stung by jellyfish and, in one crucial part of the journey to shore, was circled as prey by sharks.

It was a phenomenal story of perseverance and the motivation to get to a goal which, for him, was the shore and his family. There was no one there to help him, to cheer him on, and guide him through the waters. He had to find his way on his own and, fortunately, he did because he had the inner motivation to get to shore. Do you have the inner motivation to endure life's obstacles? In what way do you view the mountains that you face?

Sometimes mountains pop up in your life to show you how much motivation you actually have to get in order to reach your desired end. One really does not know until tested and proven, and sometimes God will allow gigantic mountains in your life so that you might exercise personal motivation to get through. How else will you be able to convince others that they can make it through their mountain or move them and how else can you truly embody a changed person? Life's mountains will always change you for the better and it requires you to not quit when you are encountered by them.

Motivation is the reason to reach for a particular goal or juncture in life. Once you have found that reason, keep it near. In my life, there has been many reasons to stay motivated. My reason may not be the same as another person's, but it is the reason that fuels my drive to succeed and move the mountain or mountains in my life.

If you have a reason to change, it will create the change you want; if you have a reason to pursue a dream, it will fuel the drive to fulfill that dream; if you have a reason to stay alive, your personal motivation will see to it that you will. Motivation is key to the change of one's identity because it is a significantly crucial part that aids in facing the many obstacles that will come your way. As a result, you will achieve your personal and unique transformation!

Chapter Twenty-Three
Soul War

There is a tug of war going on with the person that is transformed and is seeking to be transformed. This person will, at times, feel conflicted because of the lure and pull to go back into the direction you are trying to leave.

The soul is, "the immaterial part of a human being", and it sometimes longs for the old life. It's not that one does not know that the old identity was poor and of no value. However, the soul will still tend to drift in that direction and that is why one needs to be anchored, grounded, and established.

This anchoring comes from a made up mind about the changes that you say you desire in your life. A made up mind anchors the drifting soul. We all drift just further than others sometimes, and the question then becomes, can one survive the drift? The answer to that question is yes.

One can know that they are drifting when someone says, "That person is a lost soul" or "That person is out there", or "He or she is a drifter". The issue at hand is that the person's mind has not been solidified to fully implement their change or particular habit.

Such was the case with me. I drifted many times during my process of change. After my release, I drifted back and forth between lifestyles so much, that anyone who really observed my behaviors would most likely say that there was no way this man was truly sincere about change. There was an inner conflict in my mind that caused my soul to wander. In other words, my life began to wander between paths and worlds.

Some pathways were full of righteous light, while others were filled with pure darkness. I share that to say, expect the soul to be wandering especially as your thought life is in the process of being solidified.

It does not mean that one is not sincere. It's just that, when the thought life is being shaped, and when one begins to develop more of a concrete thinking about a particular thing, their thought processes will most likely tend to wander back and forth.

A person who used to drink and smoke marijuana may give up the booze, but may not give up the marijuana. They may waver back and forth using it because they may not have made up their minds on whether or not they are going to quit or not. This means that they have an unanchored soul on that subject.

Transformation does not come easy. My change has been a gradual process. This is one example from my life. When I left prison, I had been unemployed for two years. I did not work a normal paying job. I worked from time to time at a temporary agency. Some days, I was sent out to work, and some days I would not. I packed a lunch, woke up early and showed up every day, but was not guaranteed work just because I showed up.

The people at the temp agency were usually from other countries. Some did not speak English, but were looking for work and some were former criminals, like me, whose record at the time, barred me from getting a job because the CORI reform was not yet in place for Massachusetts. I really didn't want to sell drugs. I had just served an 8-10 prison sentence. I didn't want to go back for fast cash.

However, I took the risk because I needed money. One night, I went out so that I could see if I could make some quick cash selling crack cocaine. I wandered the streets and ran into a couple that was looking for crack. The guy asked me if he could get one piece for $15, even though it was supposed to be $20, but I was still willing to" take the short " despite my desperate need for cash.

A street light came on, and he noticed my face and yelled, "Oh no not my man, not my man". He recognized me from prison and knew me as a brother who used to teach Bible studies on the modular unit in MCI Concord when I worked as a kitchen worker while doing time there.

The woman that was with him was startled by his reaction and, although he was shocked to see me and couldn't believe he was out seeing me sell drugs, he bought the crack anyway.

I tell this story to say that my soul was wandering because my mind was not made up on whether I would bend during hard times and do the wrong thing or keep my integrity and do right.

Anyone seeing me out there would think I wasn't changed or sincere about it. My thoughts were in disarray because I was not anchored and my soul was drifting. I was drifting back into crime and I had a few close brushes with the law, but never was caught.

Chapter Twenty-Four
Seasons of the chameleon

As I look back and ponder my transformation, I noticed that there were times where my process was accelerated and had times where I felt stuck. I attribute this to the seasons we go through. In human development, we go through stages where our physical bodies grow and then, eventually, they level off. Similarly, seasons produce crops at certain times and, at other times, even with a significant amount of effort, will not produce any fruit at all.

I think one thing we should know and be educated on is that there are these type of seasons, spiritually speaking. Once you fully grasp the concept of spiritual growth, you can better navigate and will not be taken back by the outburst of growth and times of depressing stagnation. We go through seasons to learn how to adapt to the changes which, in turn, makes us more versatile.

There is one particular animal that represents this well, the chameleon. The chameleon is an interesting creature. They have a survival technique that depend on the situations or circumstances they find themselves in.

They possess crystals underneath the superficial layer of their skin and can alter their skin tone to send various messages. A lighter skin color projects hostility to other animals, and a more bland and dark skin color projects submission.

Many of my friends have said I'm like a chameleon because I can adapt with those who are from the streets and those who are not. My ability to adapt and find different techniques of making it through both good and bad times comes from navigating seasons and the people I meet in those seasons.

Seasons produce versatility so that you are not boxed in to one mode of operation. Some people can only operate, think, feel and associate a certain way. Part of my new identity has been to become multifaceted in the different seasons of life.

It does not come overnight, but by evolving during the seasons and learning what will work best for me and then behaving accordingly. One of my personal abilities that have come from experiences that could have only emerged through the different seasons of my life was my ability to communicate and relate on various levels.

For example, there was a season where I was in prison, so I can relate and identify with the culture and the things that come with being incarcerated. I've had seasons where I had no Income, no job, no place to stay and relied on government assistance, so I can relate to those who are poor and struggling to survive.

I have had seasons where I navigated academia trying to better myself through education, so I can relate to students that are seeking to position themselves for better options and income.

I've had seasons where I have had nervous breakdowns, uncertain of my future and my circumstance, so I can relate to those who've been hospitalized and those whose mental health is a private storm, and the list goes on and on.

Chameleons, in order to survive, need to learn to fit and adapt to whatever circumstance they are facing. Just like the chameleons, it is imperative that we learn this in order increase our ability to connect with others. Depending on how we view and respond to them is could decide if those seasons will make us or break us. Which will you choose?

Chapter Twenty-Five
The Gift of Memory

I believe that God has given man memory as a gift so that they might store information that is pertinent to future events. Of course, there are some things that we'd rather not remember or call up into our memory, like certain traumas and pains that we tend to sweep into our subconscious.

In essence, these can be good things to have in one's memory to conjure up because they represent milestones that show just how far they have come in their journey to transform themselves into a new and beautiful person, moving away from the ugliness of their past and into a new sphere and realm of being.

Your memories are stones at certain junctures of your life that remind you of, not only where you have been, but also what

God has done in the most difficult times of your life. Sometimes we realize that immediately and sometimes it's at a later time, but, nevertheless, memory is a gift.

During stages of transformation in my life, I took a stroll down the pathway of my memories, and saw the distance created and the things that happened on my odyssey. As I saw that, I was happy and pleased with my change. One such thing I call to remembrance was how I was as a person in my teenage years.

I practiced wanton violence and now, I'm more of a son of peace. This is a clear testament that something real has occurred in my life. It means that I've sincerely progressed in my journey. We have to utilize our memory to our advantage and not get a bad case of selective amnesia and forget where we came from because, to lose that means losing one's humility, to lose humility means losing a level head, to lose a level head means losing sight of the truth, and to lose sight of the truth means walking in and living a lie.

What do you remember? How is it helping you? Does it serve as a barometer or gauge of your progress or is your memory constantly traumatizing you? I think we need to pray and ask the supernatural God just how we should use our memory so that we can further ourselves. It may be that our memories represent shame or regret. Nevertheless, if we skillfully use our memory, it can be used to advance and accelerate our growth and not be kept in the inner recesses of our mind.

One example of the importance of using memory was the fighter Mike Tyson in his prime. He was always a gruesome hitter and destroyed all opponents in the ring until his infamous defeat by Buster Douglas. His trainers, Cus D'Amato and Kevin Rooney, had Mike Tyson on a number system and, when he first started out, it made him more of a boxer with a dynamite punch.

They would yell a set of numbers and Mike Tyson would remember them and then assassinate his opponent. I believe the moment Mike Tyson no longer called this system to remembrance; he became another type of fighter. Just like Mike Tyson needed the number system to be a successful fighter, we need our memories in order to have a fulfilling life. If we allow our memories to be a significant part of our lives, they will make us better and be integral part that will greatly help us in our journey.

Chapter Twenty-Six
Snake Charmer

Snake charming is an ancient thing of the past believed to be originated in India and there is evidence of it in ancient Egypt.

The snake charmers use an instrument called a pungi that seems to control venomous snakes at the sound of enchanting music. The truth is that snakes sometimes cannot hear the sound of the mystical music, but that they sway back and forth according to the movement of the charmer.

The history of snake charming is vast. Hindus believed that snakes were pure and sacred, and that those who put them under a spell, such those as that professed magical abilities and healing, were ordained and endowed by the gods to control the sacred serpents .

These snakes were and are very venomous and snake charming is no doubt a dangerous practice. I believe that God is a snake charmer of sorts because he can control the sinner under his influence and leave them enchanted by His grace.

I would say that I was cobra-like in the past. I was violent, venomous and vulgar, yet under the charm of God I am not ? . That means that God has the ability to bring the sinner under his swaying movement and, what seems impossible, becomes possible with God.

Only God can tame the hostile man or woman, boy or girl. God, and only God, is the ultimate charmer and enchanter. When I look upon my 40 years of living, at the time of writing this book, I can see that I've been tamed in certain areas of my life and I attribute that to His graces that have been lavished upon me undeservingly, yet lovingly, and because I've permitted this to occur in my life.

Change only occurs if one permits it to happen. It's amazing how many people do not permit change. Some emphatically state that they want change, and show outward signs that they do but, when the process is about to be initiated or conducted, they fight the change they say they want. This leads me to believe that they never wanted change to begin with because their heart was not ready for change.

One's heart, soul and fiber of being has to be ready for change and permit it to happen, not the way they want it to happen, but however it's meant to happen in their life. Sometimes conditioning that is negative hinders change because a person may profess change, but their disposition is to go back to the conditioning that they know.

This brings a certain movie to mind. Brooks Hatlen, a character in the movie, "Shawshank Redemption", spent 50 years in prison upon his release. He marvels at the changes made in society from how he remembers them being before he went to prison. He goes to a halfway house in the movie and gets a job bagging groceries at a local grocery store.

Brooks reverts back to his conditioning and contemplates murdering and robbing, the typical behavior of most ex-cons. However, instead, Brooks commits suicide because he cannot handle the pressures of change. This is the classic tale of one's own conditioning contributing to one's lack of progress in making change occur.

Hence, this is the reason why one must be deprogrammed and then programmed to new behaviors. This work is only done through the working of the Divine to make one's previous thought patterns different then what they used to be. This explains why the Divine is the ultimate snake charmer because, not only can he charm, but he can change the nature of a person from one way to another.

Chapter Twenty-Seven
Kings don't Compromise the Crown

One of the foes of personal transformation is compromise, and compromise means to settle or come into an agreement with something or someone and find a happy medium during a conflict, either external or internal. Early on, I learned valuable lessons about compromise and how dangerous it can be when one is trying to change their life and life circumstance.

For example, this is something more on a lighter note, but when I started to engage in a spiritual life in prison, there were those who tried my sincerity by asking me to do favors for them, like smuggle cigarettes back into the unit after going to court or stealing food from the state prison kitchen where I worked so that they could have a more fulfilling meal with the canteen they purchased from the prison canteen.

One of the things I learned was that there was always the ego at the center of them trying to get me to compromise, meaning I was always worried about what they would think of me and if I would have their approval and acceptance if I didn't compromise.

The ego always desires to be soothed by acknowledgement of some sort and is never satisfied because it always craves more attention. Also, I noticed when I did not compromise, I gained greater respect than I would have if I did compromise because it took a level of conviction and courage to not agree to negotiate my beliefs .

No matter how much one has changed or how long you've been in the process of personal transformation, compromise will always be an enemy of your progress. It does not always allow you to negotiate everything, just portions (specific) over time and eventually, because of compromise, you will find yourself in a foreign land with no idea how you got there.? Someone who knows their value and worth, or has a good sense of direction, will learn that they are royalty and value the crown they earned and won't negotiate the crown under any circumstance.

One such person that exemplifies this is John Thompson, the former coach of the Georgetown Hoyas Basketball Program. In the 90's, Rayful Edmond, the man responsible for bringing the crack epidemic to D.C., was an avid fan of John Thompson's program. Apparently, he had befriended Alonzo Mourning, who was a rising star in the program and heading for a successful career and future in the National Basketball Association.

Everyone knew that Edmond was king of a drug empire and abroad in D.C. He would show up to games to how his support and he would befriend the players, mesmerizing them with the allure of his charismatic personality and wealth acquired by illegal activity. It quickly became a known thing of Rayful Edmond's association with the team. John confronted the drug dealer and warned him not to associate with his players. It took courage to do that and not compromise because of who Rayful Edmond was.

Edmond was a violent man who typically annihilated anyone who challenged what he wanted to do. He showed just how true this was when he arranged for a pastor to be shot twelve times because he opposed him. This time was different. John opposed him and Edmond did not retaliate but quietly disappeared.

The point in sharing this story is that it takes courage to not comprise. For me, I wrestled with compromise and still do, but the fact that I wrestle means that I value my crown and don't want to lose it or negotiate it for something or someone making empty promises to me for it.

When one values the crown they have given, they learn that it's very crucial that they keep it as a symbol of who you are. Dealing with compromise is going to be an on and off battle, but, in the end, i one worth the blood and sweat.

Chapter Twenty-Eight
Black Pearls

Pearls can be found in mollusks that have a shell. The formation and production of a pearl comes from sand entering an oyster and causing pain, intense pain. The oyster deals with the irritations caused by the grains of sand by turning them over and over, and the end result is the production of a pearl.

Black pearls are a rarity because they are only found in black-lipped oysters and cannot be man-made or produced. They have in them a black-tinted nacre that show the colors of the pearl to be grey or black. The value and price for one such pearl is very high. Nevertheless, they are produced through a significant amount of difficulty.

We all hate pain and life irritations. We would rather have convenience and comfort. Yet, the Divine sends pain and irritations our way, or rather permits them, with the end result being the production of a rare and admirable result, the pearl.

Throughout my life, I've had many irritations and pain. Some have complimented me on how patient I can be and some have said I'm special and that God's hand is clearly on my life. However, these manifestations have not come without a grueling process and price.

In other words, I'm the oyster that persevered through pain and irritations and produced a rare pearl. Trials come upon us all. No one is exempt, but how we navigate and respond to them determines the end result. What are you doing with your pain?

What we do with it determines the type of person or persons we become. Because of what you been through, people will see you as a pearl and the wise will acknowledge it for what it is. We give our pearls to others when we share our pain. In my life and service, I've found that I reach others with less of what I know, and more of what I've been through .

Life rewards and approves of a process. There is no pain like the pain of disappointment and I've had my share of those.

I can remember one such disappointment recently when I was there for someone that said they needed me. I wrestled with the situation they were in because I was not sure if it was my place to be there but, because I promised them and gave them my word and I value my words because I came up like that, I was there for them in their darkest hour, only to have them betray my loyalty in the end.

I felt so much pain because I thought that this person would've valued my commitment to their cause, but instead, they didn't. I turned to God realizing that Jesus had been through the same thing when Judas Iscariot betrayed him with a kiss. Luke 22:48 says, "But Jesus said unto him, Judas, betrayest thou the Son of man with a kiss?" (KJV) It sounded like Jesus was pained by the act of disappointment.

My point is that there is no pain like the pain of not getting what you expect, the phone call, the hospital or prison visit, the doctor's diagnoses, the marriage or marriage result, the kids not turning out the way you had hoped, the job you wanted, the friend to be your friend like you were for them, the love and appreciation of family, etc.

Nevertheless, pearls are still being produced, rarities in you as a person. This is the part of your personal transformation and growth that will qualify you to be heard from by others because you have a resume of pearls for every pain that you've had in your life. For each experience of pain, there is a production and manifestation of pearls that are proof that you've survived your troubles and that you have become better because of them.

Chapter Twenty-Nine
The Giving Dynamic

The apostle Paul writes, "In everything I did, I showed you that by this kind of hard work we must help the weak, remembering the words the Lord Jesus himself said: "It is more blessed to give than to receive." (Acts 20:35). This giving does not just come in monetary form, but also in the form of giving one's thoughts, strengths, being, time, attention, and help in whatever way the situation may dictate.

I speak on this because, in my transformation, I've found that I've been called to help others with their transformation in whatever way I can play a part in. Scientists have done physical studies on the act of giving to others and it has been documented that giving reduces stress in one's body and promotes an increased quality of health. Not only that, there is the inward satisfaction one receives that surpasses the satisfaction of receiving. One mark of a changed person is the ability to give. It is a mark of change because human beings are prone to selfish desires and interests.

Therefore, one has really changed and is also really blessed when they are able to give. I recall a time in my life where at the local church I was attending. There was a great financial need during the height of a recession, and the school teachers at my church were in need of getting paid and one such teacher was in danger of losing her home.

I had some resources, not much at all, but I was moved to engage in the need and help out. I wrote a check, and the word got out of what I did. That same teacher came and graciously thanked me for my giving, wept and told me, if it wasn't for my giving, her and her husband would have lost their home and she added, "This is what the love of Christ is about." Years later, I saw that one act come back to me in a multiplicity of forms.

The giving dynamic is one thing that you cannot escape because in one's journey to change, someone or a group of people have contributed to your change at some point along the road. It is this dynamic that causes a level of reciprocity to be in demand. It is just how things are ordained to work within the laws of life.

The act of giving is a representation of the relationship between the Divine and man. It is a virtue that is of the highest kind because it is rooted and based in pure love. A dynamic is a process that is always energized and active. It never dies, never fades and is always at the helm of what you do.

So, to really be blessed is not to have a large bank account, a mansion or yacht or to be able to purchase expensive jewelry at the finest stores and to travel to exotic places rich with culture and life.

To be truly blessed, to be fully satisfied on the inside of one's being, you have to discover a dynamic, that is not of basic human tendencies and thoughts, but is one that is supreme, and is one that God possesses and makes you more like him at heart .

92415774R00117

Made in the USA
Middletown, DE
08 October 2018